the art of ~~living~~ *giving*

the art of ~~living~~ *giving*

KARLEE HAYES

Healing House
PUBLISHING

First Published in Australia in 2025
by Healing House Publishing
www.healinghousepublishing.com

© Karlee Hayes

All rights reserved. No part of this publication may be reproduced, stored in a retrieval system, or transmitted, in any form or by any means, electronic, mechanical, photocopying, recording, or otherwise, without the prior written permission of the publisher.

The National Library of Australia Cataloguing-in-Publication entry

Title: The Art of Giving
Author: Karlee Hayes
Paperback ISBN: 978-1-7641185-2-1
Editor: Vanessa Barrington
Cover and Internal Design: Heidi Glasson

Healing House Publishing is committed to publishing works of quality and integrity. In that spirit, we are proud to offer this book to our readers; however, the story, the experiences, and the words are the author's alone.

For Tim.
Who taught me how to stop, to be cared for, to truly receive.
We've laughed and cried through lifetimes,
my not-yet husband, but forever my love.
I hope everyone finds their Tim.

disclaimer

This book is a memoir. It reflects my personal experiences, memories and perspectives.

While I have tried to portray events truthfully, certain details have been altered, condensed or combined, and most names have been changed to protect privacy.

The people described in these pages appear as I experienced them during those seasons of my life, while they, too, were moving through their own seasons. This story is not written to judge or hurt, but with respect and gratitude to all the characters that shaped me. My own struggles inevitably coloured how I saw and understood those times, and it is from that place I write.

This book contains descriptions of mental health challenges, trauma, and grief that may be distressing for some readers. Please take care in reading.

This book is not intended as medical or professional advice. It is offered as a personal story, and readers should seek qualified professional guidance related to their own circumstances.

If you need support, a list of helpful resources can be found at the back of this book.

1

I was nineteen, sunburnt, and undertaking my first industry placement at Long Island Resort when I met Jake for the first time. He was in housekeeping and had been on the island for five years. I was excited, with stars in my eyes, and he was a creature of habit, set in his ways. He had tattoos of ex-girlfriends, and a nightly ritual of chips, cheese and gravy washed down with tins of XXXX Gold. Our relationship began like everything does in paradise. Light and easy, no plans. But now we'd left paradise and tried to settle back into the real world, things were losing their sparkle. Maybe it was the money problems, or perhaps the cold. Maybe it was just the strain of transitioning from palm trees to practicality.

I feel the vibration of my silenced phone buried within my blazer pocket as I weave my way through the manicured hedges lining the paths between classrooms.

"Hey Bob!" I answer.

"Ha, hey Bob!" Jake jokingly returns.

"What's going on? You alright?"

"Ah, no, not really," Jake begins. "Well, I'm fine now. Good as gold now. But I've just been sent home from work."

"What? Why? What happened?" I quiz.

"I got sick again. Proper sick. All over the suite, I'd just finished cleaning. It just came on so quick, I had no chance to get anywhere. So, I threw up all over the carpet, even on the bed. It was horrible."

"Oh my god! Jake, that isn't good! And what, you're fine now? What did your boss say?!" I fired back.

"Well, I was just about to hand the room in. She knew I was just finishing it off, and then the next minute saw me race through the corridor with arms full of spew-covered linen. She was just shocked. I told her I'd need another 15 minutes, and she barely said anything. I cleaned everything up in no time, but once I'd finished, she felt it best I take the rest of the day off," Jake declared.

"But I was fine. I felt fine cleaning the mess, and I'm still fine now. Just a headache," he finishes.

"You're going to have to see a doctor. You should do that today," I demanded with equal parts certainty and uncertainty. I knew the question that would come next.

"Where do I go?" his voice shook in the first glimpse of fear.

"I don't know. I'll have to look it up or ask some of my lecturers. I'll sort it out," I rushed, keen to end the call.

I was frustrated that I wasn't in my hometown. I'd never had to book my own doctor's appointment here, let alone someone else's. I opened Safari on my phone and began Googling local doctors. I vaguely knew I should search 'bulk billed,' even though I don't entirely understand what that means. As I continued reading and searching, my phone began to ring again.

"You right, babe?" I answered quickly when I saw it was Jake.

"It's happened again. I've just thrown up while driving home," he declared. The line was muffled, and his voice sounded shaky.

"Okay, well, let me get out of my next class and I'll come get you," I said, scrambling for words and thoughts.

I gathered myself and began the short walk back to our cottage, only hundreds of metres from the campus. My pace quickened with every step.

How does someone get a wave of sickness without feeling it coming on? It didn't make sense to me. He otherwise felt fine, working one minute, dusting the surfaces and then covering them in vomit the next. I couldn't help but compare it to when I'd been sick before. Every time I'd thrown up, I'd felt it coming, sometimes for so long I almost willed it to happen. As my steps shortened, my breathing grew shallow. *He must be very sick.*

A vision of him driving on a mountain highway, singing to his car CDs, then covering his dashboard in vomit and swerving off the side of the road came to mind. My stomach dropped and urged me to reach for my phone.

"Hello, beautiful!" Mum answered in her warm and joyous tone. "What's up?"

"How much does it cost to call an ambulance?" I heard my voice crack. I was on the verge of tears, even though I knew crying wouldn't help. Mum's tone quickly shifted.

"Don't worry about that. You just call an ambulance!" she said sternly.

"Okay, thanks, I've got to go," I said and hung up.

♥

I rounded the corner to my cottage home and was shocked to see Jake's car in the driveway and Jake pulling towels from his vehicle. I walked straight to him, my body knew what it needed before my brain could catch up. I dove straight into his arms. The hug was instant and instinctive.

"Are you okay?"

"I'm fine, me!" he assures in his thick English accent.

"We have to get you seen today. You're sick."

"Yeah, I dunno. It would be good to get something for the nausea."

We got in the car and headed for the main street of Katoomba to visit the doctor. The big gulley that separates Leura from Katoomba seemed longer than ever.

"I'm sorry, we are full, we wouldn't be able to see you today," the receptionist reasoned. We have no appointment, but I plead with her once more anyway, thinking this time might be more successful, rather than on the phone.

We head down the street from the top of the Katoomba hill toward the chemist. When we arrive, I politely speak for Jake and explain his sudden bursts of nausea, the fact that the doctor couldn't see us and questioned whether they had anything they could give us over the counter.

"Here, Jake, come over and I'll take your blood pressure," a female pharmacist signals him closer. She's tall and looks to be about 30 years old.

"Sit down here and just pop your arm out of your jumper, if that's okay?"

"Yeah, sure, at least you want to help me. They didn't want a bar of me up the road!" Jake jokes. She straps his arm, eyeing his tattoos.

"That's a lot of ink there!" She smiles, waiting for the arm band to inflate.

"Yeah, it's a lot of special work," he said proudly, rolling his shirt up to show her more of the artwork.

"Just hold still for a second, yeah?" She holds down his arm. A few seconds later, the machine beeps, and she knits her brows together as she checks the monitor. I can see the monitor: 173/115.

"Okay, let's do that once more, this time keep extra still, okay?" She holds his arm once more, peering into his eyes.

"Take a nice breath for me and relax," she suggests kindly.

Jake smiles in return, doing as she instructs.

I watch the young pharmacist await the reading, and I hope the number offered this time won't alarm her as much as the previous one seemed to. I don't know what constitutes good or bad blood pressure. I begin to search my memory for my own blood pressure readings. I can't think of any numbers. The pharmacist shifts her body weight from one leg to the other as the blood pressure monitor flashes its result. 185/124. She smiles at Jake.

"Can you just wait here while I ask my manager something?" she says, letting go of his arm. She gently offers another smile, asking him to stay calm.

The lean pharmacist carefully takes the two stairs behind the pharmacy counter to reach a mature male, who is busy with his head down, deep in thought. She nears him and quietly begins to speak to him. I can't hear what she's saying. The busy pharmacist's attention is eventually broken, and he peers curiously in our direction. He asks his young colleague a question, which she quickly responds to as he still partly focuses on his task at hand. Her response pulls his full attention toward us, and he immediately places whatever was in his hands down and begins moving toward us. He smiles at Jake as he reaches for the blood pressure machine.

"You're not feeling well, young man?" he says, restarting the blood pressure machine.

"I feel fine at the moment! Just been getting sick out of nowhere." Jake shifts in his chair and adjusts his arm into a more comfortable position.

"And otherwise healthy and well?" the pharmacist asks, wrapping the arm band around Jake.

"Fit as a fiddle, me!" Jake promotes with conviction. It's oddly reassuring. I've done my fair share of telling doctors I'm healthy, too, though I know I've got a couple of bad habits. Jake just takes it to a whole other level.

As the pharmacist waits for the blood pressure machine to inflate and constrict, he looks around the busy chemist. He smiles at familiar faces, and I'm mindful of the growing pile of scripts he has to fill.

"Thank you for helping us," I say, catching his eye. I can see the words hit him as he peers down at Jake, as if to search for a reply. The blood pressure machine beeps in response instead, and we all turn our attention to the result. 187/123. No drastic changes.

"Hmm, it's very high, young man. You really need to be seen by a doctor today," he says sternly, as though the day is young and not nearing dark.

"We've tried," I interrupt. "They wouldn't take us."

"I'll give them a call now and see what I can do," he says. He releases Jake's arm from the machine. Jake slowly begins to find his feet, but I can see he's calculating every move to stand up. Have I been paying any attention to him?

The pharmacist ducks and weaves his way through the waiting people and doesn't hesitate to interrupt the young lady serving to whisper in her ear. He swiftly takes the two steps up to his area of drugs, and inevitable piles of scripts and reaches for the phone.

"Hi Carol," he says in a relaxed tone that immediately confirms they've spoken more than once today.

"Yeah, listen, I've got a gentleman down here with reports of sudden nausea and…" he pauses, seemingly interrupted by the other end of the line.

"Yeah, that'll be him. Listen, his blood pressure is very high, and it would be good if…" he's interrupted again. He pauses.

"Great, they can do that. Thanks, Carol." His body relaxes. He hangs up the phone and begins to approach us.

"The doctor will see you this afternoon if you're able to head up to him straight away," his eyes widen to express the urgency to traipse back up the steep Katoomba hill.

"Oh, fantastic! Thank you so much for talking to them. We'll head straight there," I assure him, reaching for Jake's arm. Jake begins to climb to his feet. I watch the pharmacist watching his every move.

"And Jake, take it easy, yeah? Look after yourself," he offers kindly. He's acting like an old friend, yet all we've shared is a high blood pressure reading and his phone call to ensure Jake gets medical attention. He smiles as we walk out the chemist's doors.

We begin our uphill journey back toward the medical centre quietly. I search the shop windows as they fly past, looking for anything to capture my attention, until the strip of shopfronts comes to an end and the footpath turns into the garden front of the Carinngton Hotel. It's a majestic castle on the Main Street of Katoomba, which undeniably screams of rich heritage. On most days, I can stare at this building for lengthy stints and not help but envision beautiful ladies of centuries ago, arriving by horse in beautiful, puffed skirt dresses. But today, as I glance toward the majestic gardens, I'm interrupted by Jake's face. He catches my glance in his direction and rolls his eyes.

"Fuck me, how long's this bloody hill?" he smirks in his cheeky English way.

We exchange a smile for one another before moving our eyes back to our feet. We pass the old city bank bar, bustling with people living their ordinary mountain lives, and for the first time, I pass it with genuinely somewhere more important to be. With quick strides now on the flat pavement, we pass the new funky coffee shop, where familiar barristers smile at me as they stack their chairs for the day. Near the medical centre now, I'm so out of breath, I wonder if I'm unfit or if I just haven't breathed since we left the chemist. When I think about breathing, I wonder where my thoughts have been for the quick walk up the street. I'd been somewhere nice, I'd been distracted. But now, as we reach the door of the medical centre, I'm back in reality.

The receptionist is expecting us, and it's clear she's not got anything left to do for her workday. She immediately ushers us toward the doctor's room. The doctor, too, is packed to go home, with his bag on the desk and an empty lunch container by his feet. He gestures for us to take a seat.

"Jake, I hear you've not been well?" He says, swivelling his chair to face us.

"Well, yeah, I was sent home from work because I spewed all over the suite I'd just cleaned. I just spewed out of nowhere," Jake says as he watches the doctor strap the blood pressure machine around his arm.

"Oh dear, that's no good. And how long have you been feeling this way?" He clicks the power button on the machine, and the arm band begins to expand.

"Well, I've only been experiencing the nausea for a couple of weeks on and off," Jake looks to me for confirmation.

I begin to recount the times I'd seen him sick. I wasn't entirely aware of how many times he'd been unwell. I'd been aware of how little he'd been eating and how difficult our conversations had become, but I wasn't aware of just how many bathroom visits he'd made just to be sick, or perhaps how many trips outside for a cigarette that hadn't been a nicotine hit.

The blood pressure machine beeps to alert the doctor to another result. He wears the same face as the pharmacist from down the street, only he doesn't suggest a second reading; instead, he requests that Jake move to the bed to sit for some further inspections.

"I want to listen to your chest if I can, young man? I want you to breathe big, deep breaths from your mouth, okay?" He reaches for his stethoscope and moves toward Jake.

As Jake climbs onto the bed, I can see his balance quickly become impaired. My quick leap from my chair alarms the doctor, and he, too, reaches to catch Jake. Catching him with his hands on both of his shoulders, the doctor stabilises him on the bed. As Jake finds his balance, the Doctor gently squeezes his shoulders as though he's grateful that it didn't become a bigger drama. The massage on his shoulder is friendly, nothing more than squeezing the arm of a friend after not having seen them in a long while. The type of squeeze that confirms their presence in this world.

As he squeezes his last friendly gesture on Jake's shoulders, Jake and I both flinch. I know he cannot stand any form of massage, particularly on the shoulders.

"Oh, ouch!" Jake winces at the squeeze. The doctor's attention prickles at his reaction, and he pinches his shoulders once more.

"This?" He squeezes. Jake wriggles under his pinch.

"Yes, ouch. I can't stand massages, me!" he whips again. I can't be sure if it's Jake's thick northern English accent or his tender shoulders that's alarming the doctor.

"Oh, really? I'll need to apply a little more pressure, sorry mate." The doctor begins to pinch his shoulders. He then shifts to a pressing motion as he moves two fingers across his shoulders, then up his neck to the base of his skull. The further his prodding fingers climb on Jake, the more Jake's sensitive body reacts.

"Oh, I'm sorry, Jake, I'm barely even touching you there. I'm really not applying much pressure at all." He pinches more firmly toward the top of Jake's spine, right where his neck meets his hairline at the base of his skull. Jake locks his widened glance on me, and his eyes communicate all the possible harm he'd like to inflict on this doctor.

"Ouch, are you done now?" Jake pleads.

"Sure, I can stop. This is most probably the explanation for your raised blood pressure. Having constantly tight muscles or an injury can result in raised blood pressure. So too, prolonged blood pressure is likely the cause of your nausea." The doctor looks to us both as though he's awaiting our approval. Jake's lack of response only screams to me that he isn't too happy with the diagnosis. Jake's serious dislike of massage is not a pained neck that's causing pressure on the pumping of his blood. He simply doesn't like massages. I search Jake's eyes and plead with him to say something. The silence continues. The doctor is in charge again.

"We can't be sure without further tests. I'd like to do some bloods, so I'll arrange an urgent blood sample for the morning. Do you know where the pathology clinic is?" The doctor glances between us both.

"It's down near Centrelink, right?" The words race from my mouth before the backlash does.

"Yes, that's right. Get that done tomorrow, and I've booked you an appointment back here to see me on Monday," he says as he passes the pathology form to me. I glance at the form and make no sense of the several abbreviations listed. Feeling rushed, I check to see if I have any lasting questions, but the doctor has already switched off his computer and is reaching for his bag.

Feeling hurried and confused, Jake and I begin to make motions to leave. I wonder what Jake will say when we reach the comfort of our car. I understand that while he's been sicker than I understood these past weeks, it's the fact that he's hidden that from me that truly explains how concerned he is. Hurried to my feet now, I just can't help myself.

"Just so you know, it's not a tight neck that is causing this," I begin. I know we're leaving, and as the doctor has his arms balanced with his Tupperware and drink bottle, I know he doesn't want to help us anymore.

"I can't help until I have the blood results. Just get that done and I'll see you Monday."

2

I returned to my big cottage home in Leura to try and at least organise an overnight bag for Jake. I'd managed to keep my shit together while I was at the hospital, but now, standing in my tiny bedroom, which was actually an office I'd converted into my own space for some privacy in a home full of fellow students, all Asian girls, I felt myself beginning to spiral.

How long is a stay in hospital for someone who's just been told they're in complete organ failure? How many pairs of jocks do you pack for someone who's just been declared as the most toxic living human the doctors had ever seen have a blood test? Will he need jocks? Or will he be having surgery and be dressed in a gown the whole time? How do they fix someone with organ failure? Do they cut them all out and replace them? Hoodie, I'll get his hoodie, that will surely keep his top half all cosy while the rest of him lies under hospital blankets. A phone charger is a must; he'll need it to contact me. And to scroll through Facebook, to kill the time. How much time will he need to kill? How long will he be in hospital for? Maybe I'll pack more clothes.

I begin to pace back towards his bag of clothes that have been somewhat semi-permanent in my small university-provided room.

Why not take his whole bag? It's basically packed already, and that way, he'll have everything. I grab the bag and pivot to leave the room. *No! That's stupid. What if it all gets lost or stolen when left unattended at the hospital?*

I change direction again and place the bag back in its usual spot. As I pivot once again, cold air brushes my cheeks. I left the front door open, thinking I'd be quick, but I haven't been quick; I've just gone in circles.

Just stop.

I come to a halt in the middle of the room and reach for my phone to see how long I've been. 4.40pm Saturday, 16th May. I need to hurry up, I need to get back to the hospital.

Think Karlee.

I begin toward the kitchen in search of a tote bag, but halfway down the hallway, I think of all the half-filled tote bags in my room. I pivot once again. Feeling another rush of cold air, I think of the wide-open door again, that's letting all our warm heat out and the cold Blue Mountain air in. I pivot again, racing for the door. I pull it shut. As the door bangs closed, I remember I'm not the only one who lives here. As I begin back down the hallway, Reece's door creeps open, and she carefully pokes her head. She's been sleeping. Why do Asians sleep so much, I think.

"Karlee, are you okay?" she asks sleepily. "Is Jake okay?" she asks more gently. I lock eyes with her and feel the emptiness in my stomach. I see the same worried eyes that tried to help me this morning. The same eyes that asked the same question hurriedly, as she stood at my bedroom door when I couldn't wake Jake. The same eyes that asked, "How can I help?" as I screamed and shook a lifeless body.

Reece grabs my attention as she emerges from behind her door, her tiny body draped in laced pyjama threads. She stands in front of me, her arms crossed and eyes stern.

"Karlee, is Jake okay?" She tries again, this time with a straighter, braced stance. I hadn't asked myself that question.

I'm here to get clothes for him, and I need to be quick.

"Karlee, has Jake died?" She asks firmly, taking one soft step closer to me.

"No, no, he's about to get taken down to Sydney. He is toxic; all his organs failed. I don't know anything else, I don't know what's going to happen! I don't know what that means! I don't know how they fix someone with failed organs? What will they do?" I begin to realise how much time I'm wasting when I start pacing toward the bedroom.

"I just need to get this bag of... Ah! Bag!" I pivot once again to the kitchen for a tote bag, then remember all the bags in my room once more. Frustrated now, I make a sharp direction change right in front of Reece. Reece unfolds her stick-thin arms from across her body and reaches for my fast-moving body.

"Karlee, stop for a second!"

She holds both of my shoulders with her cold little hands.

"Take a second to think. It's okay. What will he need? Just some clothes for the next 48 hours, and what? A toothbrush, his phone..."

"Ah! A toothbrush, good idea." I exhale a breath that feels

like it's been held hostage in my body all day. I stare into Reece's eyes, and I can see her genuine care.

"Don't overthink it," she says gently, squeezing my shoulders and lightly shaking my body.

"You can take anything you forget another day."

Her advice is so logical that I let go of another breath.

"You're right," I sigh.

"Go get packed, okay?" She shakes my body one more time. Eyes still locked on hers, I nod and swallow the last of my confused thoughts. I peel myself from her hands and head toward my bedroom.

As I step back into the small, cosy bedroom, I can't help but stare at the single bed that only hours ago held Jake and me, tightly wrapped in each other's arms, asleep. I stare at the unmade bed and begin to replay the moment I woke that morning. I watch this vision unfolding from a perspective high up on the ceiling. It's not apparent why or what woke me before our 8am alarm. We were waking early this morning for the blood test, as directed by the doctor. But I see in the replayed vision of myself that I wake and stir, then, in my calculation and careful motion of turning over to face Jake, I watch the immediate alarm on my face and the panic in my movements. I watch as I untangle myself from the doona cover in a swift movement whilst coming to an upright position. The quick motion in my vision spurs me to catch my breath in the present moment. Standing in the middle of my room, staring at the unmade bed.

"Shit! Hurry up!" I say out loud. I reach for my phone to check the time.

4.47pm. I need to hurry up.

I pour the contents of a tote bag out onto the leather sofa, then frantically dive through Jake's bag. I grab jocks, trackies, a hoodie and his toiletry bag. Feeling organised and certain now, I dive for his phone charger that's plugged into the power bank by my bed. I throw it into the tote bag and begin heading toward the door.

As I near the glass French doors, I catch sight of Jake's beloved Rosary beads hanging from the door handle. The beads are only ever off his neck when asleep. Every night before bed, he carefully removes the beads from around his neck and hangs them ever so meticulously from the door. Not one to go to church or have ever read the Bible, but if ever asked about the beads, he'd say, "I don't go to church, but I have faith. Someone has always looked after me."

I grab the beads from the door handle.
It's now more than ever he needs faith, someone to protect him. Whoever it has been throughout his life. Holding the beads, I think again about how precious they are. I don't want them to get lost. I go to place them back on the door, and I'm met again with hesitation.

No, these are important; he'll want them. I'll pack them. I begin to put the beads in the bag, and touch my phone's only button to check the time. After all this hesitation and too-ing and fro-ing with beads, I've got to be wasting time. I glance at the time. 4.49pm. I'm certain the beads should stay safely at home. I pull the beads once more from the bag and go to place them back over their door handle, and just as I do, I'm met with a feeling unlike anything I've ever experienced. *Death.* My head is totally clear, no frantic thoughts. Just one: death. It's strong, and sure, and suddenly I don't feel rushed anymore. Is that it? I wonder. Just like that, he's dead, and somehow, I've felt it. The heavy feeling had interrupted me from hanging the rosary beads on the door handle. I go to hang them again when I'm interrupted by another sure feeling.

I need to wear them.

I drape the beads swiftly over my head without another thought. I calmly wonder now what will lie ahead of me if Jake is dead. I'm not worried; there's no point in being worried. I'm not rushing to get back to the hospital anymore. My head is clear, and all that's present is death. And as though the veil between this living world and the other has been slightly lifted, I've managed to catch a peek at the sensation of what follows this living experience. Nothing, it's still, no tension in your body as your breath struggles to move through, no chaotic thoughts ricocheting around your head, no two places to be at any one time. Death is so sure, so certain, and doesn't require any further action. Death feels exceptional and inevitably calm. It's not scary at all; I'm not scared. This feeling of death doesn't sadden me. Rather, it comforts my entire body, as though all of the pressure and stress has been lifted. The time and the pressure of moving quickly have gone. If Jake is dead, there really is no need for me to worry; there is nothing I can do at this moment.

I finish packing and begin to make my way out of the house, down the long hallway, before a voice of reason or logic politely interrupts my empty head. I start to bargain and convince myself that it surely isn't Jake that's dead, but the deep knowing and hollowing sensation still has me believe that someone has died. Perhaps it was the lovely old gentleman lying in a bed next to Jake in the emergency ward. More convinced with this theory now, I think of his dear wife, who sat with him holding his hand. The lovely couple that smiled sweetly in a way to send comfort, condolences and warmth to us, when Jake's stretcher was wheeled into the ICU ward. Perhaps the old gentleman is the one who has died. It seems more realistic to me now. Of course, it's not Jake who has passed.

As I near the nurses' desk at the Katoomba emergency department, I'm greeted by a face that smiles as she recognises me. She immediately rises to her feet and assists me through the waiting room doors. At this point, I know Jake must be okay. As I begin toward Jake's bed, I'm pleased and ever so slightly surprised to see the elderly couple next to him. They catch my eye and smile warmly, and this time, the degree of warmth is at a point that has me sure of the fact that they've gotten to know Jake, and by association, me, a little better since I've been gone. They're calm and pleased to see me. They hold joy as though they might just burst out laughing. As I continue around the corner, I finally spot Jake, and I understand now why they're about to laugh. Here he is, sitting upright with a styrofoam cup of coffee in one hand and a plastic stick imitating a cigarette in the other. He puts the stick to his mouth and takes a deep inhale, as he would of a cigarette.

"Ahhhhh!" He exhales with a smile across his face. I can't help but laugh. Everything feels calm and under control. He's clearly been well looked after in my absence, and there's a sense of connection between Jake and the elderly couple that makes it feel as though you've just stepped into a country football league's huddle at half-time. Everyone has played the same first half, and it's only camaraderie that will see them through the next half. Jake continues to dramatically take a sip of his coffee, then a drag from his plastic cigarette, which is followed by smiles and giggles from all who are in witness.

"They wouldn't let me out for a cigarette, but they gave me this plastic one and it's actually pretty good! It's got nicotine in it." Jake excitedly shares his newfound plastic ciggie.

Everything is calm here in the small emergency department. A new man arrived since I was gone, a motorbike accident, and he sits holding his arm across his body, nursing either a broken arm or shoulder. I look at all the faces of the people within the emergency department. Half of them are patients, and half are their loved ones. As I scan the faces and search each pair of eyes, I can see the same kind of emotion mirrored in the faces. The patients are all somewhat peaceful, relieved of any pain, comfortable, and in a state of acceptance. There is nowhere else they need or want to be at this moment. The pain or worry that caused their visit is all too fresh in mind to be anything but thankful for help, grateful for pain relief and acceptance that this is the best place to be right now. For whatever reason, they've landed in the hospital. There's no reversing that, there's no undo button, and they've accepted that.

The faces of the loved ones, however, are scared. There's no calm for them yet. The pain from earlier in the day is still vivid. I searched the eyes of the woman who was with the man who had a motorcycle accident. I wonder if she's replaying the accident in her mind, or if she's replaying the phone call for help. As I search her eyes, I wonder what she had to cancel today to be here. Her plans have inevitably changed. I think about the business of young adults. I feel the difference between us, the younger people in the room, and the older couple next to Jake.

While they may have had their plans interrupted by the visit to the hospital, it's unlikely that their plans were too severely disrupted. However, I think the likelihood of their life returning to normal is far less than for everyone else in this room. There's a degree of inevitability that they're somewhat equipped for the ill health that old age brings. I stare at the sweet old lady sitting next to her lifelong partner. I think of how the last decade of their life, leading up to this point, would have hosted thoughts about who would need to stay well for whom. Which one of the couple is healthier, and who will outlive whom? I imagine their wedding day, and I wonder how young they were when they made promises to each other, in sickness and in health. Well, here it is, the sickness that old age has brought them, to the person that they vowed to support through it all. A sickness that we spend our whole lives unknowingly racing towards. Wishing days away between now and the weekend, now and the holiday, until we get a full night's sleep free of an unsettled baby's cry. Wishing away days until there's X amount of money in the bank, or our next promotion arrives. Days that all went too quick. Now their time nears its end, or worse, never returns to full independence again. They must be prepared, though, I think. The aged lady smiles as she gently pats the hand of her sick husband. I'm not prepared for this, though. I have no idea what the next chapter will look like for Jake or me.

3

I excuse myself from Jake's bedside and wander out into the waiting room, and then outside into the cool evening air. I reach for my phone and, as I search its contacts for one name, I will for her to answer, like I've never willed before. Murmuring a prayer-like wish that not only will she answer, but she can help me tonight.

"Hey, Paula!" I'm filled with fleeting joy as I hear the line pick up.

"Yooooo, K Dog! What's happening?!" There's a symphony of not only her good energy, but Mafalda's, too. I'm immediately relieved and relaxed at the sound.

"Girls, I need help." The words escaped with a degree of certainty that shocked me.

"Talk to me, what's going on?" Paula's tone is direct and comforting.

"Jake's sick… Really sick. He's in the hospital. He's about to be taken down to Sydney tonight, and I just don't know what to do or what I need to do. I don't really know why I called…" I pace the small sheltered entryway of the Katoomba hospital.

"Oh my god, K! We'll come to you. We'll come help. Where are you now? We'll get our shit together and get on the next train to the mountains."

"Ah, thank you. We're still at Katoomba, but we've been waiting for a medical transfer for hours now, so it should happen soon. All his organs failed. It was horrible, he's been getting…"

"K dog! Don't worry," Paula interrupts my unravelling. "We'll come now. Let us get organised and we'll be sure we're on the next train from Central," she assures me.

"Thanks, girls. I don't know what time he'll be getting taken, so I don't know where I'll be when your train gets here."

"K, don't worry. You message us if you're about to leave Katoomba, and we'll figure out the best station for you to meet us at. Don't worry about that yet, okay? For now, we need to go and catch the next train, it's in 15 minutes."

"Oh, awesome. Okay, sorry, yes, you go. I'll keep you posted. Thank you so much, Pau." I say with a crackle in my voice.

"K, don't even, anything for you! See you soon!"

♥

Despite my mum telling me to never touch my phone while driving, I reach for my phone, swipe to unlock it. I'm already looking at Paula's contact, so I hit call and switch the phone to loudspeaker.

"Hey, K dog! How ya going?" Paula answers quickly.

"I'm alright, I'm on the road now, Jake's on his way to the

Napean." I hear Mafalda mumble in the background.

"Alright, we're going to quickly do the math and tell you where to pick us up from. How was Jake when he left?"

"Yeah, he was fine. He was pretty much back to his usual self, which is alarming. He's been functioning like this for so long, he's just used to it."

"Springwood. We'll meet you at Springwood station!" She says sharply.

"Got it - the little town with the hippy shop?"

"Yessss, Hayes!" Mafalda interrupts down the phone line.

"Okay! See ya's there."

I followed closely behind the ambulance that carried Jake until an amber traffic light separated us. Wet and miserable, I realised I hadn't even sorted my car's music before I set off. I listened to the rain, the ushered sound of car tires on wet roads, and my squawking windscreen wipers straining to wipe quick enough. The oncoming car lights glisten and blur the wet windscreen, and with all the compromising conditions stacking up in my head, I can only think of my mum. I can hear her worry. It's as though she is back in the passenger seat, and I've got my L plates on. I can hear her anthem of nighttime and wet-weather driving instructions. Leave a bigger gap between you and the car in front of you. Go a little bit slower, and make sure you light up your brake lights well in advance for the car behind you. All of it over and over again. I can even feel her reach for the car's dash or handles when I take a sharp corner, as though she's being thrown around in a rally car. I'm confused now if it's her worry I feel, or my own. I've intentionally not updated her with the transfer down to the Napean hospital, because I don't want her to worry. Paula and Mafalda know where I am; they know to raise the alarm if I'm not at Springwood station anytime soon.

As I turn off the highway, I thankfully navigate the unknown entrance into the township, which sits just off the highway and within perfect line of sight to passengers on the train. I breathe in relief that I've managed to locate some free waiting bays right near the station exit, dimly lit by the orange streetlight. I turn off the car engine and leave the accessories on as I reach for my phone and the aux cord to get the music going. As I'm rustling around for the cord, I hear the train. It's leaving, so the girls must already be here.

As soon as I look up, I see the girls pacing down the steps of Springwood station with urgency. Mafalda spots my car first, points. A wave of spritely energy washes over both of them. Arms involuntarily spring above heads, smiles across their faces, a big hipped thrust from Paula's Filipino hips, and a quick, sharp, loud "Holla!" from Mafalda's petite Portuguese body. The joy is contagious, and right there in the street of Springwood, any onlooker might mistake the three of us for a reunited family embarking on a holiday, or a bridal party of hens about to drink themselves silly. I sure don't think we look like three girls faced with the uncertainty of human life or what the next hours will bring.

Paula reaches me first and embraces me, no more lovingly than anytime she hugs. It's always firm and full of everything. The hold hangs for a moment longer until the shuffle of two little dancing, impatient Portuguese feet. Paula's hug begins to squeeze the tears from my eyes, and takes any words on my lips completely away. I can only shrug my shoulders and offer a forced smile to the girls between their hugs.

"Aw, come here, Hayes. It's alright, we're here to help." Mafa wraps her arms around me and lets out another comforting, "Aww, Miss Hayes." Suddenly I'm met with urgency again as I feel the emotion begin to feel at home.

"Right. We should keep moving." I break the hug.

"Let's do it, I'll drive," Mafa demands with a little clap and points to the driver's seat. We begin to pile in.

"You okay to sit in the back, Paula?" I confirm heading toward the front.

"Um, of course, K dog. Please take the front," her certainty made me realise it was a stupid question. Of course, she'd let me take the front seat of my own car when my boyfriend is knocking on death's door. With the closing of my Honda CR-V doors and the buckling of seatbelts, Mafa swiftly turns the key and carefully wraps her hands around the steering wheel.

"Ahhhh Paella, my beautiful friend!" She cries, and all of us are instantly taken back to happier mountain adventures of last year, when we first met at The Blue Mountains International Hotel Management School. Paula and Mafa were second-year students, familiar with the school's workings and, more importantly, the local surroundings. I was just a first-year student and new to the area. A close friendship was quickly forged. And Mafa had often taken the responsibility of being designated driver of my car, as not many had vehicles in the mountains, and I was still on P plates, meaning we couldn't all go to the station bar in Katoomba and legally have one drink, then drive home. Mafa, however, had her full licence. Her good driving skills and confidence behind the wheel were easily explained by life experience growing up on mopeds and cars in her mother country. I trusted her with my car and my life.

As we pulled onto the highway and began to pick up speed and head south towards the Napean hospital, I realised and appreciated the task the girls had signed up for. Beginning their journey hours earlier at my call on a later Saturday afternoon in Sydney, journeying mostly the whole way to the Blue Mountains, only to jump in a car and head back towards Sydney once more, for an undetermined amount of time.

"Thank you so much for coming to help. I already feel so much better," I announced, turning around to look at Paula in the back. Simultaneously, both of their hands reach for me, Mafa reaching over and squeezing my thigh, and Paula's hand squeezing my shoulder.

♥

The steady flow of drunken and drug-affected patients begins to decrease, and the waiting room of the Nepean emergency becomes eerily cold and quiet. Since arriving, we've watched the changing of shifts among staff, minor injuries come and go, and we've seen security guards make their presence known to aggressive patients. We've still not yet seen Jake move into a bed. I've spent the evening getting buzzed through from the waiting room to an empty corridor, where Jake lays in and out of sleep on an ambulance stretcher bed. The corridor holds another three patients who are all too ill to be left in the waiting room, yet haven't been moved at home in the wards. With every ambulance arrival, the sliding doors at the end of this corridor rattle open and a big gust of cold air from outside smothers the already sensitive patients. While the cold air is harsh and unrelenting, it always brings through a pair of lovely paramedics, sometimes with or without patients. They always greet the corridor fillers with a smile as they politely thread themselves through a space that is not fit for storing patients and certainly not their loved ones. Another rattle of the doors brings an even cooler gust of wind and a very joyous paramedic wheeling a stretcher.

"Phewf! Brrr!" It's clear he feels slightly awkward and a bit embarrassed to see a room full of people.

"Winter is certainly coming!" he declares with a smile.

He's right. It's the early hours of Sunday, the 17th of May. Just 2 weeks shy of winter. I lean right over Jake as the joyous paramedic threads his bold self and his patient through the corridor. Now aware of the time, I'm worried just how long Jake has been without food or drink.

"You haven't eaten anything all day," I say, staring into his tired face.

"Nah, but I'm alright. I've not done much all day, have I?" He shrugs.

"Oh yeah, I suppose. So, are they still preparing you for surgery now? Surely it'll be some time if they don't even have a bed for you?" I ask, hoping he's had further updates since I've been on my trips, so I can take a seat in the waiting room.

"No idea, I haven't spoken to anyone since that brief visit from the nurse when you were here." I can hear a slight bit of frustration creeping into his voice.

"Oh, gosh, okay. Well, we're just going to have to wait, I guess. Want me to get someone's attention and ask about some food?" I look around for any faces willing or able to help.

"No, don't worry, I'm all good. I'd just prefer to try to get back to sleep. You should go home. I could be here for a lot longer still. It's been... what? Five hours in this corridor?"

Jake makes a valid point. Our time in the corridor has been so long now that we're not expecting to go somewhere anytime soon. I had stood for an hour awkwardly tucked against his stretcher when I arrived just after 10pm. As he drifted off to sleep, I assured him that I would just be next door, sitting in the waiting room for a bit with Paula and Mafa. The more hours that dragged on as I danced between the corridor and the waiting room, the more comfortable we became with the fact that he wasn't going anywhere soon.

"Well, I'll let you try to get some sleep again, and I'll head out and maybe attempt the same in the chairs," I say gently and positively, as I tuck the paper thin crunchy hospital blanket up and over his shoulders, right up to his chin.

As I walk back out to the waiting room this time, I can't see my two incredible friends. I reach for my phone to see a text.

'We've gone to rest in the car for a bit, Hayes, call us if you need anything!' I feel bad for the girls, and I decide I'll head out to the car to find them. As I wander outside the emergency department doors, I'm greeted with the chill and fog of an almost winter morning. It's quiet and cold. I briskly move past all the cars that have a dew settling on their windows and move quicker as the air finds my skin beneath my layers. I spot my car and see the glow of a phone light within it. Calmly, so as not to startle my caring and exhausted friends, I speak as I near the car.

"Yooo hoo!" I imitate Mafalda's usual serenade.

"Hola! Miss Hayes!" Mafalda sits up from the horizontally

reclined driver's seat, and Paula shortly follows in the passenger seat. I climb into the back seat as the girls reposition and turn their bodies to face me.

"Any updates?" Paula asks hopefully.

"Nope, nothing. He's still just out in the corridor. I have no idea how long it will be. You girls should head home. We could be here until tomorrow at this stage."

"Oh noo. No, we'll be making sure you get home at a reasonable hour, Hayes. We want to stay here for you. But… we are getting hungry…" Paula says with a giggle, as though they've been conspiring a plan.

"Oh yeah?" I wonder, as I divide my acquiring look between them.

"Yesss… There's a Maccas just around the corner!" Mafa gladly declares, holding her phone to my face with the maps app open. "Let's go for a little Maccas run, Hayes! What do ya think?" Mafa's body itches with excitement.

"Aren't you a vegetarian?" I laugh.

"Yes… But there's no meat in hot chippies! Olaaa!" Mafalda dances in her seat, as Paula and I inevitably catch the wave of her contagious energy.

"Yeah, let's do it," I say. "There's nothing I can do in there at the minute. Jake will call me if he needs me." I check my phone once more to ensure it's on loud, as the girls sit further upright and begin buckling up. As I do the same, I think about poor Jake.

"We can't tell Jake we've gone to Maccas! It's his favourite, and he hasn't eaten all day!" I plead from the backseat.

"Aww, don't worry, our secret. K, have you eaten anything today?" Paula bargains from the front.

Her question prompts me to relive the day once more. I see a flash of the morning and the urgency that woke me. I fast-forward through the time waiting in Katoomba Hospital. I see

Reece grabbing my shoulders in the hallway, and then the next thing I know is Springwood station, late at night, picking up the girls.

"Oh, no, I haven't. I haven't eaten since…" I cast my mind back to Friday. I had left uni early to try to get Jake some help at the doctors. "I haven't had anything since lunch on Friday!" I was shocked.

"Holy! Miss Hayes, well, you definitely need to eat. Maccas isn't the best… But it should make you feel a little more human!"

I began to think about how I was feeling. I was surprisingly calm and unbothered. I think about the number of things that are out of my control right now and begin to wonder just why I'm not stressed. There's been so much happening, and so much out of my control, that there's no place for stress. The possible outcomes are nothing but fictional stories I would be completely making up, and therefore, too unbelievable to convince myself or even worry about. I genuinely have no idea what's going to happen, and I can somehow accept that the unknown is truly peaceful and comfortable right now.

"You know what, come to think of it.... I'd murder a burger!"

♥

As I watch the passing trees begin to defrost at the first kiss of sunlight out the passenger window, I wonder how much of a hangover is actually due to a lack of sleep and a messed-up digestive system.

"I feel hungover!" I declare, casting my glance across to a very

THE ART OF ~~LIVING~~ GIVING | 39

attentive Mafa in the driver's seat. She's clutching the steering wheel at a perfect 10am and 2pm position, and her calculated blink as she finds her words tells me she's concentrating hard to keep this vehicle safe.

"Are you going alright, Mafa?"

"I'm all good, Hayes. But I reckon I may need some good tunes, hey Pau!" Mafa cries out to Paula in the backseat, who wakes from her dazed stare out the window.

"Oh yeah, let's do it!" Paula reaches toward the front for the AUX cord.

What comes next is the opening notes of our most-played song in the mountains. The song that makes me think of the three most carefree girls at the Blue Mountains International Hotel Management School of 2014. Unphased always, there wasn't much convincing needed before you'd find the three of us piling into my car and heading for a coffee trip or a beer at the station bar, and always with this song at full blast. As though it were a sacred ritual to remove ourselves from where we've just come from and submerge ourselves into the very moment. If the song got played early enough, before we'd all begin to ramble about our day or the class we just had, the route would naturally change from the direct to the scenic. And, if heading for coffee, the choice of cafe would change from the nearest to the farthest.

"We're a thousand miles from comfort," our tired voices began in harmony.

"We have travelled land and sea." I begin to wake up to my surroundings and the day that I'm living. Mafa reaches for the volume dial and turns it up with a smile.

"But as long as you are with me, there's no place I'd rather be."

For a song that had been played over and over, today I felt like I was listening to its lyrics for the first time. Today, I felt I'd lived every minute of the last twenty-four hours. I fully felt loud and clear the notion of truly feeling unstoppable when you have the right people in your life. As the last few notes came to a close, I was amazed at the energy that had been conjured together in the car. I ever so much as glanced at Mafa, and she smiled in return, and then, turning around to Paula, who was already winking at me.

We walked into my warm cottage and made our way down to the end of the house, where my converted little sunroom/office, which holds an awkwardly tucked single bed, was located. The morning sun beamed through the lacey curtains. We all sat on the couch in a collective feeling of 'what now?' It was only 10.30am. We were tired, needed showers, cold, hungry, and still without any kinds of answers for Jake's future. All we knew was that he was in a bed, in a ward, and although the ward was filled with head injuries that looked like something out of nightmares, he was comfortable and would soon have the opinions and care of professionals.

"How about we go for a big nutritious breaky, then come back for showers and watch a movie on the couch?" Mafa promoted with enthusiasm and conviction. The girls eagerly looked to me, and I realised now in great relief that they were planning to do only what I felt like today, and weren't heading home to Sydney anytime soon.

"That sounds perfect," I said, springing to my feet with a surprising jolt of energy.

I glanced at the garden outside, and immediately thought of the garden bed that Jake would usually piss on, rather than heading into one of the shared bathrooms in the cottage (which weren't really shared; they were en-suites within the proper bedrooms of each girl, except me, the only one who didn't get an ensuite.) I stepped closer to the window to look at the bush that Jake had pointed out, humorously, wasn't thriving under his morning relief habit. I considered how the disintegrated shrub and evaporated, crater-like soil had surely been a clear sign that he was unwell. I stared out the window and must have looked rather upset, because the next thing I felt was a hand on my shoulder, gently squeezing.

"Come on, Hayes, let's go have a good feed!"

4

We file back through my cottage home doors with full bellies and slowing movements. It's an awkward hover in the living room as none of us has the energy to do anything. No one knows quite what to do next. We're full of a hearty breakfast, and we've all slumped our bodies onto the couch in front of the TV. Mafa still has the most energy, helping me to dictate the next move.

"How about you go get in a warm shower? Put your comfies on and then settle here for the rest of the day." She makes it sound so comfortable that I'm convinced it's the best thing to do.

I pull myself upright and head toward my room for some clothes. As I walk into my small bedroom, I look at the unmade bed and the sprawled belongings from the upturned tote bag in my room. It's a mess. And as I recount the steps of frantic packing and what caused all the mess, I'm again watching yesterday's wake-up scene. The vantage point isn't from my physical eye line, it's again from a higher point in the room, from the ceiling. The vision replays of me stirring from my morning sleep, entangled in Jake's lifeless and heavy arms, when at some point through the stirring, a wash of fear and concern took over my body, and I untangled from the doona. I sat upright in the bed. The vision stops there again.

I continue through my room and decide to make the bed, hoping it might end the recurring vision, or at least deliver more of the story. Not seeing anything, I pull the crumbled sheets taught and fluff my pillows. Next, I search my room for my tracksuit pants and dressing gown. I collect my pile of clothes and head back down the hallway.

I reach Reece's door, who, due to her kindness, holds the bathroom I've been using. Whenever I use any other bathroom in the house, I receive nothing but a glaring eye from the other girls for entering 'their' room. I knock at Reece's door. No answer. I gently and quietly twist the creaky door handle, thinking Reece might be sound asleep as she often has a habit of sleeping at odd times in the day. As I poke my head around the door, I lean even further to catch a glimpse of her bed. She's not there. I let go of the tension in my body that was holding me quiet and tiptoeing. I open the door to her ensuite and head in. The bathroom is so cold that the fresh air on my face wakes me from the cozy, comforting temperature of the rest of the house. Not wanting to delay between getting undressed and getting into the shower, I turn the hot water knob on in the shower to begin the long process of heating the water in the cold mountain pipes. I then take a seat on the toilet. To save time, I begin undressing as I empty my bladder, untangling my pants from around my ankles, and removing my top half. The shower hasn't begun to show signs of warmth, so I end up reaching for my mobile. A Facebook notification awaits me, so I take the bait and open it.

Unconsciously, I begin scrolling the platform that is still predominantly filled with posts of people from high school, a scattering of updates from old Long Island colleagues, to old hiking buddies and even some of my old mixed netball teammates. The next update I see is from Alex, a friend from netball. She's updated her profile picture. It's an old snapshot of her with Dylan, another teammate we both played alongside.

The photo looks as though it's been pulled from the depths of a family album. The two of them red-faced following a winter game, leaning into each other with grins ear to ear. They're in oversized hoodies over their uniforms, hair wild from a combination of sweat and rain. The whole picture radiates the familiarity between close family friends and the buzz that follows a cold morning game. It's clearly a cherished image, the kind of photo you hold onto because it captured something you didn't realise would matter so much later.

I scroll beneath the photo to see several comments. Love heart emoji after love heart emoji, a few comments with a broken heart emoji. As I continue to scroll, I begin to fear the meaning behind the post. I continue to scroll the emoji-filled comments in the hope one of them will be more illuminating, and then I see it appear: 'He's going to live on through all of us.'

My stomach drops. I think of Dylan. Memories together surface quickly. They're rich and vivid in my mind. We hadn't been especially close. He was younger than me, part of the team, but always on the quieter side. Still, we shared one encounter that bound us together in a way words never did.

He had a mate on the team who could be relentless, always making fun of him in front of everyone. To anyone else, it might have seemed like harmless teasing, but sometimes I felt it went too far. One evening at training, after listening to yet another round of 'jokes' that felt quite raw, I snapped.

"Oi, you know it's hard to tell if this is a joke at all. You've got nothing but bad things to say about him, which actually just makes you look like a sour, unlikeable prick. I have no idea why Dylan even puts up with it."

"Whatever, Karlee, mind your own business," he fired back sarcastically.

Immediately, I got fired up. How dare this kid suggest I was being nosy and overstepping my place? I gestured to the rest of the team, my voice sharper now. "Well, it is actually my business when you are constantly humiliating Dylan in front of everyone. It's not at all funny or clever; it's uncomfortable to witness."

The court fell silent. I glanced at Dylan, and he gave me just a look. A spark in his eyes. A flash of gratitude. I took a breath. Everything is still silent. I realised in that moment that Dylan probably allowed their relationship to get to that point, and that perhaps I didn't understand their mateship. However, that look was enough to assure me that sometimes, the jokes weren't funny. His boisterous best mate shot one final blank look at me, slightly shook his head and walked to the other end of the court. Dylan followed.

After that night, Dylan always made a genuine attempt to greet me. He'd look me straight in the eye, sometimes nod, with sincere thanks and a smile.

And now, this quiet kid is gone. I couldn't believe it. It was clear that this news had shocked many. I watched the comments continuously add to Alex's photo on Facebook. They were becoming increasingly descriptive.

'Thinking of you at this time, Alex.'

I needed to confirm it was real. I stand up and proceed to scroll through the contacts in my phone for Dylan and my mutual close friend Chloe. I spot her name and call her. Only when I hear her shy 'hello' on the other end of the phone do I fully comprehend what I've just decided to do. I've called someone who's grieving the shock of the passing of their friend.

"Hey, I'm sorry, I just had to call to check that it's real?" I blurt frantically as I move naked around the bathroom.

"Yes, it's real. I still can't believe it, though," she says in a monotone voice that backs up her words.

"What happened?" Her voice had made me brave enough to ask. I walk toward the hand basin and the fluffy green mat beneath, to find some relief for my feet on the cold bathroom tiles.

"Not sure entirely. At work."

I place the phone down on the edge of the counter, ensuring its speaker volume is all the way up, as I grab hold of the hand basin with both hands.

I roll my head up to look in the mirror. As I do, there's only one thing I see. Rosary Beads draped around my neck. The rest of me is entirely naked, with prickled and dry skin. I stare at the rosary beads, and no words make it out of my body. I relive the frantic push and pull of leaving the Rosary beads safely behind or packing them for Jake. I relive the to-ing and fro-ing before I remember the feeling, the feeling of death. The knowing that I had to wear the beads. The peace that came to my frantic mind. The assurance that whatever comes after our time living is entirely peaceful and quiet.

I pull the Rosary beads up and over my head, and I'm now holding the cold silver cross. I feel the heaviness of death in my whole body. The sensation isn't as calming as it felt yesterday.

"When did it happen?" I ask Chloe.

"Just before he knocked off yesterday", she responds faintly. "Around five apparently"

"Yeah, that sounds right." I cut myself off, realising it's not the right thing to say. "I'm so sorry, Chloe. Thanks for filling me in. I just can't believe it. I should let you go. Go easy on yourself, okay? You make sure you all get together with all your friends and look after each other," I plead with her.

"Yeah, thanks, Karlee. We will. Speak soon."

♥

I can feel my heart beating faster as I navigate through the skinny streets of Newtown in Sydney. My hands are clammy on the steering wheel, and I plead to see a car park, and one that I can get into. I curse myself for not practising parallel parking more. I frantically search for a gap in the cars, and I realise I'm driving further away from RPA hospital. As I crawl past a line of angled parked cars with the noses faced into a park full of Sunday afternoon drinkers, I stare intently at the cars for any action, before I see the white reverse lights of a vehicle light up. I quickly hit the brakes, then check behind me for any close-sitting cars that may have missed my quick reaction. A small hatchback quickly reacts behind my car, and I brace myself for a blasting horn as I politely cast a wave over my shoulder. Nothing. The car simply continues down the street.

I wait for the family car to slowly begin reversing out of the car park, and at this point, I see the green sign explaining that the car park is restricted to just 2 hours.

"That'll have to do," I murmur under my breath.

I drop my phone in my bag, grab the drink bottle from the cup holder, and tuck it away as well. After climbing out of the car and locking up, I slip the keys into my bag and start walking. But about fifty metres from the car, I've convinced myself the handbrake isn't on. The thought of my car rolling into the park ahead creeps in, and suddenly, I'm not sure how bad the future could really be. As I walk back toward my car, I'm conscious of the fact that I have $75 to my name, a very sick boyfriend and don't need any other headaches right now. I peer through the window to see that the handbrake is on. I consider any other possible inconvenience that could happen, and think about having left my headlights on. I race to the front of the car to check. They're not on. I slowly begin to walk away from my car once more, genuinely attempting to think of any possible inconvenience that I could cause myself. The only one now I realise is a parking ticket. If I don't hurry up and get to the hospital, I could be at risk of one of those.

I set off with determination in the direction of the hospital.

As I walk briskly, I realise just how far away I parked. If Jake is coming home today, there's no way he can walk to the car. I'll have to race back to the car and pick him up from the hospital entrance. As I walk through the hospital doors, I check the time. It's taken twenty minutes out of my two-hour allocated car park to get into the hospital. So, at most, I can only stay for just one and a half hours before I'll have to consider moving my car or leaving.

I approach the information desk at the hospital and announce who I am and who I'm here to see. The woman kindly directs me to the renal ward.

"You can walk to the end of this corridor and take the lifts up to level nine, or you can head up the ramp if that's quicker."

The journey sounds like a mission already, considering the twenty-minute walk it's already taken to get here. I near the lifts to see many others waiting. One lady watches as the lift lights up another level that clearly isn't in her favour. She rolls her eyes and, with a huff, she heads hurriedly toward the ramp. The ramp proves immediately that it's practical, and when I look at the ramp, I realise its architectural magnificence. This ramp spirals around a dome-like new extension that almost resembles art. Gruffly, I decide to take that route and question if the money spent on this extension could have been better allocated. Perhaps alleviating the cost of parking near the hospital to ensure anyone hard done by didn't need to walk twenty minutes to a free park. As I pity my circumstances, I consider that most probably everyone in this building, and its visitors, are hard done by. But at least they can afford parking.

Almost dizzy from the spiral mission toward the sky, I reach the doors of level nine. Above the open doors is a sign that reads 'Renal Ward.' I search my basic biology knowledge and wonder if I have ever heard of the word 'Renal'. It's sounding familiar and as though it does encompass the organs.

As soon as I walk through the doors, my immediate reflex is to bend my neck and peer into each room and search the faces for Jake. It doesn't take long for me to spot him.

Worriedly, I lean close to Jake for an embrace, and the moment I return to upright, I'm not at all sure what to say. I pull my phone from my bag to check the time, and I feel exhausted as I calculate that it is a three-hour journey from my cottage home in Leura to Jake's side here in the hospital. Having been in close contact while apart, I feel I'm fairly well-informed and need not ask how the surgery went.

"How are you feeling?" I sigh as I pull the nearby visitor chair beneath my body.

"Fucked. I'm ready to go ho.." he begins, only to realise he doesn't really have a place to call home right now, as he bunks with me in my single bed in my university-supplied accommodation.

"I'm ready to get out of here," he corrects, before he pushes down the blanket from his torso, and begins pulling up his white hospital gown to show me his new addition.

"It's a PD catheter," Jake says, looking down at his heavily taped stomach. Exhausted, I still don't have much to say.

"I don't know when I'll be using it, though."

I feel some quickly moving breaths get caught in my chest as I search for any response to this foreign tube that now dangles from my boyfriend's body. I search my head for the logic of what the letters 'PD' mean.

"I still think I'm coming home today." Jake hopefully suggests.

"Are you sure that's a good idea? You don't look very well. And what happens next?"

No sooner do I blast Jake with my questions; a team of people enter the room across the hall. Suddenly, armed with the awareness of my surroundings, a lady in the bed opposite Jake catches my attention and politely calls out.

"You'll be able to ask all of the doctors those questions," she smiles, attempting to comfort me, and softly nods her head in a gesture to the team of people across the hall. I smile politely back at her and reach for my phone to check the time. I worry once more about the restricted car park.

The team of doctors make their way over to us and kindly positions the curtains around us for a bit of privacy. They start by asking Jake how he's feeling after the surgery, and he energetically responds.

"Yeah, good, I'm feeling good," he assures them.

"Well, the sooner we get you home, the sooner we can get the Renal unit out to start you on dialysis at home," the confident young doctor confirms. As I get tripped up on the mention of 'home.' I wonder what they mean and how disruptive dialysis at home will be to my housemates.

"What's this dialysis going to look like? Like, how is he meant to do this from home?" I innocently ask.

"Oh, Peritoneal Dialysis is one of the most easily managed forms of dialysis. It can be performed at home and throughout your day, allowing you to maintain a better lifestyle. Jake will be back to his usual routine and can perform dialysis at work on his lunch break if needed," the doctor confirms. He sees the shock and doubt settle across my face, as I still wonder how this all happened.

"This method uses a simple solution that Jake can now feed into his abdomen, sitting in the Peritoneal cavity, which is like the cage and space around his major organs. This solution will stay in his body between exchanges, and it works to draw all of the toxins out of his body, instead of his kidneys doing that work. As they're no longer working." He sees the alarm settle on my face before continuing once more.

"The Renal Services team will be able to explain that all a lot better, and they'll be the ones setting you up at home with everything you need."

I look at Jake's face to see how he's handling this, and he's unalarmed.

"So, I'll be right to go home today then?" Jake asks.

"Yes. Absolutely. We'll prepare your discharge papers, and you can head out as soon as you have them. Shouldn't be more than an hour," the doctor smiles, before him and now what appears to be students all begin to make their way out of the room.

I immediately think of the car again, parked far away and begging for a parking ticket. I realise I shouldn't think about it too much, because it's bound to happen if I think about it. I vow to think of something else, and then I'm immediately thinking of the influx of information that I just learned about my boyfriend's future, my future, and the cage encasing our organs, that's called the peritoneal cavity. I unlock my phone and begin to frantically Google the word.

"It's okay, babe. The Renal service people will be teaching us everything we need to know." Jake captures my attention and ever so calmly assures me not to worry.

I read and read my phone, as Jake rests on the bed. As he tosses and turns to get comfortable, I can see across his face that he's not at all well. I worry that he's not well enough to come home and that I'm not equipped to look after him. I watch his discomfort once more as a nurse enters the room.

"Hi Jake! You're ready to go home, I hear?" She affirms the ridiculous idea joyfully.

"Yep, sure am," he says, immediately wiping the grimace from his face.

"Great, well, I'm just arranging your medication with the doctor now, but otherwise you're right to get dressed and ready to go," she says, referring down to her clipboard.

Jake begins to position himself upright when a thought rushes to his mind.

"And what do I do with this big tube that now hangs from me?" He raises his hospital gown slightly.

"Oh, I'll help you get that anchored and taped up for now. The Renal nurses will provide you with some snazzy accessories when they visit you at home."

I watch the young nurse bring her tapes and scissors to Jake's bedside, as I evaluate how positive everyone else seems here today. As though it's a plague that I'm immune to. Everyone has been so certain and assured that everything is fine and there's nothing to worry about, but that's all I can manage to do. I campaign in my head that I know Jake better than them all, and that's why I know more than they do. Yet, I'm met with a sheer respect for the medical industry. They certainly know a lot more than me, and I should probably trust them much more. But, I also know now that my boyfriend was operating on very little kidney function for months, and in that state, somehow managed to turn over large suites at The Hydro Majestic, in record time, as though he was some foreign phenomenon. It's me who understands how well this guy can conjure a believable facade.

I look up to see Jake's face staring into mine as the nurse manoeuvres the long tube that has been newly inserted into his side. Jake winces ever so slightly before he casts me a smile. His face maddens me. He's on the same campaign to get out of the hospital and go to this elusive place called 'home.' Yet, we don't have one. If it's anyone's home, it's mine, yet I don't even have a bathroom that I can freely use without the torment of the Asian girls making me feel like I'm using something of theirs. And here I am opening their home to a man they hardly know. Who now has to perform dialysis at home and live a life of uncertainty. I just don't see how that's a 'home' we can be excited to return to. I don't see how that's a home that Jake can rest and recoup in.

"Okay, that all looks good now. You should be right to get changed, and I'll bring in your medication and discharge papers once I have them. It shouldn't be too much longer," the nurse says as she removes her blue surgical gloves.

"How's that sound? Any questions, Jake?" she asks as she picks up her tape and scissors from his bed.

"No, that sounds good to me." He confirms.

As the nurse leaves the room, Jake begins his attempts to get off the bed. It's clunky and new, as though he's never gotten out of a bed onto these legs before. I rise with immediate concern and get closer to catch his fall. I can't yet tell what hurts or why he's not moving so freely.

"What hurts?" I ask as I take hold of his arm securely.

"My tummy feels like it's about to explode," he says, putting his hands to his back and stretching his lower back.

"Are you sure you don't need to stay here any longer?" I ask quietly, in a way to have a private conversation in his shared room.

"No, no, I'm absolutely fine, I just need some proper rest. I haven't really had a sleep since Friday." Jake's mention of time makes me reach for my phone. My car park is up.

"Okay, well, I should go and move the car. My space is up. Do you think you'll be ready by the time I get back? In about twenty-five minutes?" I ask hurriedly as I help Jake find some clothes to put on.

"Yeah, surely. I'll follow them up and make sure," Jake assures me as he begins untangling himself from the hospital gown. "You go get the car, I'll get things moving."

I begin my hurried walk all the way back to the car. As I exit the hospital doors onto the inner Sydney streets, I'm met with a waft of smoke from patients in hospital gowns. I thread myself through their smoke-filled air quickly and try not to make eye contact in case my hate of the scent is too obvious. I maintain the hurried pace as I catch the red flashing pedestrian man, and race across in front of vehicles inching to the line, ready to go. Jogging now, I begin to get more nervous about a parking ticket. *I wonder how much that will be. Whether or not you get the opportunity to pay it later. Maybe I can find some money for it somehow...*

I spend the long mission to the car urgently changing pace between a brisk walk and a jog whenever I think about arriving in line of sight to the car and seeing the parking instructor just writing up a ticket. I rearrange my falling bag across my shoulder and think about how sticky this city is. I pull at the front of my shirt quickly to produce a slight breeze between my shirt. As I do, a nearby passerby clears from the path entirely to allow me to pass. I smile politely and see her alarmed face. As I clock her reaction, I realise how frantic I must appear. Considering this, I slow my hurried pace once more, trying to comfort myself.

I'm already late, so I've possibly already got the ticket. I should just relax.

As I turn the next corner, the park full of Sunday boozy picnic goers is in sight, which means my car is almost in sight too. My toes take to the curb eagerly, as I look both ways before crossing the street. Now, on the footpath the nose of my car sits on, I search the windscreens of all the vehicles. No other car has a ticket. I'm hopeful mine won't have one either. The closer and closer I get to my car, the more details I can make out. Windscreen wipers, with nothing underneath them. Yet, it's as though the less evidence of the ticket, the more convinced I become that I must have one. *Perhaps it's just put somewhere else.* I reach the car, and frantically check all the windscreens, the tires, and lastly my door handle. Nothing. No ticket.

"Lucky…' I murmur under my breath. I unlock the door with urgency and throw my bag across into the back seat. I turn the key to start my reliable car, and as I turn the ignition, I'm still convinced that I might have somehow left something on to flatten the battery and inconvenience myself once more. On the first turn of the key, the car starts as usual. I catch myself in unrealistic worry and try to shake it quickly. *Just drive.* I put the car in reverse and quickly find the friction point of my manual car that's on a downward slope. The car moves quickly and smoothly away from the curb, and as it does, I'm overwhelmed by noise. The sound of a screeching horn that must be blasting for my attention. I quickly hit the brakes.

I frantically perform my head checks and search the mirrors for any indication of what's gone wrong. I look all around, as though there could be a number of reasons someone would blast their horn at me, and it could certainly have come from any direction. Nothing. I can't see anything. As I stare into the rearview mirror, I catch sight of a frantic white van that takes off sporadically, throwing his middle finger in the air to the other side of the road. I'm startled, but thankful the incident isn't my fault. As I realise I'm holding onto a breath, I release my foot from the brake, and allow my car to roll back into its park, and find sanctuary with its nose to the curb. I pull the handbrake on. As I take my clenched hands from the steering wheel, I untangle my feet from the pedals too. Placing my hands in my lap, I take a big breath. As I exhale, I feel the warmth of tears coming to the corners of my eyes. Another breath in brings more, just not as frantically. I consider crying and calling my mum, but I just can't bring myself to explain that I'm just wanting to cry because a car horn beeped and it scared the shit out of me.

I'm not even sure that's why I want to cry. Maybe I'm just relieved all the bad things I was certain would happen haven't happened. It's nothing to cry over. My mum certainly wouldn't think there's any point in crying over situations that haven't happened. I'm fine. I'm totally fine.

I take another deep breath and think about what needs to be done now. The only thing I need to do is drive safely to the hospital entrance, pick up Jake, and get safely back to the mountains. That's all, nothing else. *I need to stop worrying.*

I slowly near the hospital and search desperately for any carparks. The entrance to the hospital is confusing. A big sandstone building with paved areas full of smokers in hospital gowns, nursing staff on their phones, and visitors milling around. With so many people, it's hard to tell whether the paved area is built for people or cars. There's a van parked in the area that suggests it could be for parking. As I search closely for any further indication, I realise it's now too late to turn in there anyway, I'm passing the hospital.

I'll need to make some kind of U-turn and find somewhere else to wait for Jake. As I pull up at another set of red lights, I reach across for my bag in the back seat of the car. I dive my hand into the bag and search for my phone. As I feel it in my fingertips, it begins to ring. It's Jake. Illegally, once again, I answer the phone and switch it to speaker.

"Hey, I'm just about to reach the front doors. Where are you?" Jake loudly says, as he reminds me of the tone I need to speak to him in.

"I've just driven past, I'll need to turn around and come back," I say clearly.

"What?" Jake asks. *Gosh, his hearing is so bad.*

"I've just driven past. I'm turning around. Can you cross the road and wait on the other side? Out the front of the cancer building?" I scream.

"Oh, yes! Okay! See you there, Bob!" He humorously plays.

I end up missing all the possible turns I could take to turn around and end up travelling right around the block until I reach the cancer building, where I see Jake waiting. I scan the street signs in front of him and cannot see any indication that I can stop there. I check the rearview mirror to confirm there are barely any cars behind me, since I entered back onto this road at the red lights. We'd better be quick.

I pull over illegally, and Jake moves slowly to the vehicle. I have no choice but to rush him. So I hurriedly and dramatically move my hands for him to see through the window, as though I'm scooping him towards me. The moment he's in the car, Jake breathes a breath of relief, as I do the opposite. I instantly search the mirrors for my gap in the stream of traffic that is now manoeuvring their cars around me. I find my opportunity and take off.

As we get out of the small suburbs and onto the familiar road to the mountains, Jake sees the alarm in me subside. He looks over to me from the passenger seat and smiles.

"I can't wait to get home for a cigarette," he declares with a cheeky tone. "I know that will get things moving," he motions to his stomach. "Then I'll be good!"

"You haven't shat? When was the last time?" I bark.

"Not really. I can't remember. Maybe before going into hospital…"

"What! That's not good. Why didn't you say anything? You should have told the nurses; they would have given you something," I argue, as my heart rate begins to climb again.

"I'll be fine once I get home. You know what it's like," he assures me.

I'm alarmed he is still looking forward to going back to my cottage home, which offers us only a single bed to share, and no bathroom of our own. I think he's forgetting the death stares we receive whenever we try to use a bathroom, as though I'm not even entitled, even though I pay the same amount as the other girls. Yet, Jake, who isn't meant to be there, feels that he'll be able to relieve himself once he gets back there. I'm now dreading the foreseeable future.

As we begin to climb the mountain, the roads get increasingly familiar. Jake wakes from a nap and clenches his stomach, letting out a moan. He repositions his legs beneath him, pulls his hands up to under his head, then drifts back to sleep.

As we pull into the cottage driveway, I'm reflective of how much time has passed since Jake has been here. It feels like months have passed since we both woke up here together. I can tell Jake is thinking the same things as his eyes scan the big building and the trees.

"Can you believe it's only been five days?" I say, looking at him.

"Mental," he offers quickly before speaking more urgently.

"My gut knows how long it's been!" He reaches for the door handle. We get out of the car, and as he opens the back door, I interrupt him.

"I'll get your bag, you head on inside."

I make a trip around to the other side of the car, grab his frantically packed overnight bag, and head indoors. As I walk through the house, I see Reece's door is ajar, and I'm certain that's because Jake has snuck into the bathroom. I continue down to my end of the house, dropping the bag in my small room and finding a moment of comfort on the couch. I kick my shoes off and raise my feet onto the raised end. As I breathe in the comfort of my little room with many soft furnishings, I close my eyes.

I wake from a dazed state when Jake walks through the door. As he carefully pulls open the door, he follows the door handle with his eyes, and I know what he's in search of.

"Oh, here!" I say, quickly reaching from under my shirt for the Rosary beads.

"I didn't want them to get lost, so I wore them." I search his face for partial relief, but I only see some distress.

"You feel better?" I ask, pulling myself to a seated position on the couch.

"No, nothing happened. I'm heading outside for a smoke," he says, fossicking through the overnight bag.

"You need to eat some prunes!" I say with conviction, like I would to anyone. Only my suggestion is met with a blank stare, because I surely know this English bloke hasn't eaten a single piece of fruit or a vegetable in his life.

"Well, you might have to if it gets any worse," I warn.

"I'll be fine after this." He holds his rolled cigarette gently in his hands and slightly raises it to the sky as his body moves with joy beneath it.

"Okay, grabbing some fresh air."

5

It's been five months. Five months since Jake first got sick, and somehow everything has changed without really changing at all. We've traded one city for another, packed up our lives and moved to the other side of the country. We moved to Victoria Park, just a stone's throw from the Perth CBD, and a short fifteen-minute drive to my second university placement at Adina Apartments. But sickness doesn't care about new postcodes or fresh starts. Jake is still really unwell.

There's a particular brick that I trace with my eyes for hours on end, to kill the time. The brick is on the other side of our small living room, in direct line of sight when I'm sitting on the couch. The black 'click clack' couch that Jake and I picked up from someone's hard rubbish and carried for over a kilometre for the sake of getting a couch. Having a comfortable couch can make a significant difference in your life. However, this couch rarely made any difference; it was so uncomfortable. I'm sitting rigidly, hard as a board; every muscle is activated to hold me upright. My legs are struggling to fold up underneath me because every one of my muscles is sore. I haven't stretched or exercised in a long while. The brick wall had this one brick that was set slightly further in than all the rest. It was badly painted white, pasty and rough, much like my skin that hadn't seen much of the outside world in a long time. I hadn't done much else but travel between my car to the hotel, hospital and apartment building door.

Quite honestly, I can't even guess how many hours I've spent staring at this one particular brick. I trace it with my eyes over and over again. Starting at the top left corner, my eyes follow to the right corner, down to the bottom and continue along until I've traced the rectangle brick with my eyes. Start again. I am just being, I am just existing, I am wishing the time away. The only way my current nightmare is going to end is the death of my boyfriend. I've accepted this long ago. Several hundred brick tracing laps ago. I simply need to keep going. Keep looking after him, keep going to work so I can pay the exuberant rent for our bottom-floor brick dungeon apartment, which by location means our small courtyard is the ashtray of the thirteen balconies above. I have to keep trying to get Jake into hospital, keep my cool as medical professionals continuously put the responsibility back on me and send him home to be in my care. Keep trying to fumble my way through, scared and feeling stupid because I don't know enough, I don't know where to get help, and since my last phone call with mum, I feel I have no one to talk to. My mum's words down the phone line begin to replay in my head.

"You told the Government you're in a de facto relationship? You shouldn't have done that!"

"Well, yes, mum, we live together, we're in a relationship, and I'm keeping him alive. I can hardly claim that I'm..."

"He should be getting on a plane back to England, where his own family can look after him. It's not fair for you to..."

"Urgh, Mum! That's just not an option. He is not fit enough to fly. No airline would accept him. Or he'd die the moment he gets home. His mum and family don't have a cent to their name, let alone the capacity to care for him."

I replay my words as they fire at mum, leaving me breathless and struggling to stand in the long line of struggling citizens outside of Centrelink.

"Well, someone else should be looking after him. It's not fair. You're too young to be dealing with this, and you've got uni and placement, and it's not fair that you have to give up your life. There's got to be someone else who can care for him." I replay her pleading for my own innocence.

Working all day meant that I'd either be heading to the hospital late afternoon or lining up at Centrelink to report or attempt to fix up our payments and reporting requirements. At this point, we're solely living off my casual income. Jake's Centrelink payments have stopped because he doesn't meet his requirements. The requirement is that Jake needs to visit the job office to get help with finding a job, yet he couldn't make the appointment, because he couldn't get out of bed that day. He was admitted to the hospital again instead. Then, because he didn't make the appointment, he didn't get paid. For the same reason he couldn't get a job himself, he's sick, the last thing he needs is an appointment to try and help him get a job.

The type of dialysis that Jake is on was painted to us as the kind that would give freedom to a young couple. This dialysis was supposed to mean that we could live our normal lives. It required more frequent attention; however, it could be performed from home or wherever. It was presented to us as the cure that would allow us to get back to living normally. It almost seemed glamorous. I, a hardworking hospitality and non-smoker. If Jake had to step away for twenty minutes at least, it was for something that wasn't harming him, unlike the smokers taking their breaks; he was giving himself health by doing dialysis at work. My aching legs still hold a quiet resentment toward every smoker who's ever worked in hospitality. I would have loved just five minutes regularly to rest.

As I trace the brick again, I can hear a distant yet close enough domestic dispute.

How nice it would be to have the energy to get worked up over something. How nice it would be to have some kind of fire and passion to cast such horrible words from your mouth at someone else.

I try to envision Jake and me ever reaching such decibels, impossible. He held his pain so quietly, in fact, he held his pain in pure silence. His arms even folded across his body in an attempt to hold it all in. His right arm would fold across his small frame, and his hand would take hold of his left elbow. His left arm bending to hold his aching forehead. He would either sit in that folded position or he'd lie in and out of sleep in bed.

♥

It's always a long walk of twists and turns to any renal unit. Nepean Hospital, Sydney, Westmead, Royal Prince Alfred and the darkest and longest walk, the path I trekked most, Sir Charles Gardiner Hospital, Perth, Western Australia. Renal patients are prone to infections, so flowers aren't allowed. In fact, there's really no joy in these units at all. No matter how hard I tried not to glance into the other rooms of patients, I couldn't help myself. I always found myself looking at their age or their visitors. I search for anything familiar.

Do they have answers? Can they relate? Do they know how many millilitres of toxin-filtrating Icodextrin are in their partner's abdomen right now? Do they analyse blood pressure results as an indicator to predict how long this stay will be and how many lonely nights they will face on the lounge, tracing the bricks?

The patients are all dealing with undoubtedly lengthy visits, and gone are the days of 'Get Well Soon' cards. The balloons are long popped. This is a dismal place, fluorescent white, ordinary, and low energy. It's normal life now for most of these over sixty-year-old patients.

I would often get excited when a young nurse walked in. Though often no sooner had fresh air filled my lungs, it would escape as their nerves became too obvious. And if they held a glucose reader, Jake and I would tense. A simple tool, yet the most painful prick of all. Jake's ability to recover from surgeries, have tubes inserted into all different parts of his body and barely flinch was truly incredible. He'd fold his arms in the same way he always did, like he was holding everything together, including his forehead. When a veteran nurse was de-tubing or about to prod him, his hand would slightly shift its angle on his forehead. Slightly covering his line of sight. But if a young nurse enters the room, everything changes.

We'd both tense. Immediately, we'd check the time, hoping it wasn't on or approaching hourly observations. *Please just be here to check the urine output. Just Panadol. Anything but the finger prick.* But if a young nurse arrived for obs (observations), dread would swell. Jake's arms would leave their folded position and fall stiffly by his side as if he were about to restrain himself. His hands would lie so close to the railings, ready. Ready in case she fumbled. And some days, when things were exceptionally bad, I would sit forward in my chair and prepare myself to be able to deflect any pained, uncontrollable, flying punches that might escape from Jake's pincushion arms. No sooner would they draw blood; the other free hand would be so tightly clutching the bedside railings. Holding himself down to the bed, no hands to cover his winced face or his lips that whispered 'Fuck me,' in his thick northern English accent.

I enter the room and he's lying on his side, facing me, with his PD catheter stretching and trailing from his stomach, up and over his sharp hip bones. The tube that carries the life-saving glucose syrup in and out of his body several times a day has been carefully placed so as not to pull too much tension on the tape dressing at the site in his stomach. The arm of his underside folds beneath his cushionless body. A body so skinny my eyes so often trace lines like connecting the dots between the points of his major joints. I can just see his arm from under the gauze-like blanket, tucked, poking out near his pinched and gaunt stomach. His elbow looks so pointed and sharp, surrounded by skin that no longer owns muscle. The skin, so slender it bleeds the thick black ink of his tattoos into one another.

I've seen all these tattoos from all kinds of angles, and I

can complete the picture within my mind, even by seeing just millimetres of the sleeve. I follow the rosary beads along his slim arm up to the prominent point of his wrist bone. The nodule on his outer wrist is so rounded that I can't remember if I've ever seen his or anyone's wrist look so pointy. *High school lunchtime. Wrist comparisons. No one's wrist was ever that pointed.* His hand cups his cheek as he rests. Despite everything, his lips look so plump. Poised together in the same gentle lip that may just catch the tears that want to fall from his eyes, but never do. His face is lightly shaded as it rests against his upper arm, which drapes over the cold metal bed frame. His other hand, which somehow holds enough space for a cannula on top, holds onto my own plump, cushioned, and strong hand. The stark contrast between these two clenched hands holds enough light and shadow, enough story, to inspire the masterpiece of a fine art sketcher.

Voices at the door jolt me from my gaze. Jake stirs at the shift of my hand. I always get excited at the sound of someone at the door. A schoolgirl's response, like we're about to be rescued from a dull class. The voices belong to two young nurses, with slender bodies, one in purple scrubs. An agency nurse. That means they're short-staffed. She smiles, makes eye contact, then boldly declares:

"You're going home today, Jake!"

I exhale hard, and although there are thousands of thoughts and layered feelings racing through my brain, none reach my lips. It's then I realise. It's more comforting for him to be here. I used to feel lonely and a bit scared on nights when I was alone or walking down the long, dimly lit brick hall from our garage to our unit. But now, the idea of having him home is far more frightening than that darkness. Nothing is as scary as the thought of having him home.

Will he be able to get up and go to the dentist to get the work done to be eligible for the transplant list? Will I need to dash to the shops for him before I go to work? Will he be able to get out of bed to perform dialysis? How do I stay focused at work while Jake lays ill at home? How long before I'm packing his things to come back in here?

"The doctor reports that you've just got to continue dialysis every four hours," she interrupts my spiralling thoughts.

"We are already doing that!" I spit, no more spiralling, just anger.

"This is ridiculous. The dialysis isn't working; he only goes longer than four hours in the middle of the night to catch some sleep."

The purple scrubbed stranger fumbles with the clipboard at the foot of his bed.

"We're already performing dialysis every four hours, and we're back in here every ten days. It's not working. It doesn't work. Look at him."

Jake begins to adjust himself from his slumber, facing the reality that he needs to get out of this hospital bed and relocate home. Every movement looks painful and heavy like a marathon runner lacing his shoes for another race.

"He cannot get to appointments to get the transplant because he's so sick, and then he winds up in here, and we're rescheduling all of those appointments again. We need help. He needs to stay here." I slump back in the chair, exhausted, as though I've already lived the upcoming week of my life in advance.

"You've just got to perform dialysis every four hours," the purple stranger announces coldly, detached.

Rage. Seething, blood-boiling rage involuntarily swallows my body. I can't do anything but shake my head and stare at my hands. Plump, capable and shaking. *She's just a messenger.* The thought gives me a strange sense of power. *But she's a shit messenger.* I repeat her words over in my head again and again.

She didn't even say sorry. She didn't empathise at all. Why the fuck is she even doing this job? Several faces flash through my head. Those who have treated, pin-pricked, advised, dressed wounds, and removed tape. Their faces are all too similar. Eyes glazed, mechanical-like movements. Just doing their job. *Have any of them empathised?* Or is that just my job? It's always me. *I'm the one whispering sorry. I'm the one rubbing his hand. I'm the one whose face winces when they fail at landing an IV.*

No one else cares like I do. But I do. I will. I have to. I know I will somehow manage the week. I have to; there really isn't a choice.

6

My job at Adina Apartments Perth is a clean, normal, routine-driven sanctuary from my otherwise sterile and bleak life. A sanctuary that allows me to get up, shower, do my hair, a light face of make-up, and suit up. A straight navy skirt, atop legs with stockings, a red button-down shirt, and a beautiful blazer, tailored to accentuate the curvy hips of our team. In fact, the uniform suited those with hips more than it suited those without. The few boys in the front of house team all looked fine, but nowhere near as beautiful as us girls. The process of getting ready, leaving my brick dungeon, travelling ten minutes in a car that plays my favourite Jack Carty 'Break Your Own Heart' CD on repeat, parking underneath the convention centre, then walking through the clean and well-manicured driveway to the front desk, manages to completely take me away from survival to exceptional service mode. The moment I walk through the glass sliding doors to find the smiles of the shift that has been on before me, I'm in a completely new world, a world I love. I love my team. They are calm, unique, and all very good at their jobs. Our boss Emma offered me my role as a guest service agent for my second-year placement. Emma had been the one to provide me with my first placement on Long Island, and when she later relocated to Perth, we stayed in contact. So, when it came time to organise my second placement, she made room for me on her team in a heartbeat. Emma knows Jake, too, and she is the only one in these walls who knows exactly how ill he is. When I went for the job, I explained how much I enjoyed coming to work to escape the world I was holding together at home. I loved getting dressed up, following our systems and procedures, and delivering exceptional guest service to anyone who approached our front desk. I prided myself on always being on time. Twenty minutes prior to shift start time is on time. Ten minutes early is timely. Arriving at the minute my shift begins is late. I'm thankful for the education and standards that my university has set for me. So far, it's seen me stand out among every team.

My first placement on Long Island was only for six months, and although I was hired by Emma, a man named Craig became my manager a short time later. He landed on the island, watched and listened to everything for weeks, and then quickly promoted me to a management position. Although I tried to explain there wasn't much point as I'd be heading back to university soon, he wasn't concerned. He said he needed me to hold Palms restaurant to my high standard through Christmas and the busy period.

I didn't feel I was anything exceptional; I just felt aligned with the standards we were trained to uphold at the Blue Mountains

International Hotel Management School. We wore stunning navy suits, with silk blue and orange scarves tied neatly at the neck and tucked into the collar of our crisp white shirts. Every strand of hair was slicked back, and we wore just enough makeup to look polished. We held ourselves with professionalism. We turned up early, listened intently to industry professionals and absorbed every lesson passed down from our trainers. At the end of the day, we took off our suits and lined up with our mates for the Asian buffet at Yu & Mi or dressed up for a fancier meal at the fine dining Chambers restaurant. We lived and breathed the hotel industry, preparing to represent the college out in the real world.

I had done myself and the university proud with promotions and accolades in my first placement. But here, on my second placement, I'm doing something even more difficult; I'm making myself proud. Managing everything outside of work is enough. The personal demands, the worry, the care. But arriving at every shift energised, groomed, and on time? Well, that was something else entirely. I had never been late. Never called in sick. Only once had I swapped a shift when I couldn't leave Jake alone. I was careful not to make a habit of it, but I'd learnt the schedule of my staff's lives intimately so I could request a favour when I knew I'd ultimately need one.

I walk around the front desk and, out of habit, glance at the pile of registration cards in the middle of the desktops, indicating how many arrivals we have coming into the hotel today. It's an average day, fifty guests or so, I assume at a glance. I continue past Emma's office, waving to her as she's on the phone. I file to the corner of the back office, where there's space to store away our bags, and a little fridge for packed lunches. I habitually spray on some perfume and stow it back in my bag. I reach to check my phone one last time before switching it to silent, and then I fossick in the small pocket of my handbag for my name badge. I can't feel it. An immediate pit is formed in my stomach. I've left the badge at home. I can now see it, in my mind, sitting on the dining table. *Why did I not put it straight back in my bag, like I always do?* I continue my frantic search as I pull out several items from my bag. My wallet, water bottle, and loose paper. No name badge. I begin to feel the eyeballs of the back-office staff watching me as they witness my increasingly frantic searching. I search my bag, even though I know my name badge isn't in there. I keep searching to mask my disappointment. I never forget things. Especially not my name badge. I'm always ready early with time to spare, so that I never get stressed or rushed. Great, I'm now stressed and rushed. My uniform begins to feel tight as I crouch down to empty the contents of my bag on the floor. *I really want this stupid name badge to be in my bag. I know it's not.* Just as I begin sensing defeat, I'm interrupted.

"Ohhh, what's up, Jessica?!" Our sweet reservations agent, Geoffrey, jokingly interrupts.

"Oh, I know, looks like that's me for the day! Silly me!" I look to the microwave for the spare name badge. Jessica. A name of jovial banter across the room. One that has always been a bit of a laugh. If you forget your name badge? You're Jessica. If anything ever went wrong, blame Jessica. Can't find something? Jessica must have moved it. A joke that has been enjoyed by most members of staff by now, except for me. I've never been Jessica. I've never forgotten my name badge. At university, not having your name badge on would warrant an immediate fine from the student representative council members. Your badge is a part of your uniform, and I've left mine at home.

In defeat and immense frustration, I reach for the spare badge that hangs stuck to the side of the microwave. The ordeal has frazzled me, and I'm so upset that with all the moving parts and distractions in my life.

I never mess up. But I have today. To others, it might seem trivial, but it isn't to me. *I don't make mistakes like this.* I'm thankful to be at work twenty minutes early, because the lump in my throat isn't dissolving in the back office. I head to the bathroom.

Upon my return, I weave myself behind the backs of my fellow front desk members who have just had an influx of people walk through the door. I watch our boss Emma rise from her desk at the sight of the many people waiting, and we smile as both join the desk team, looking like special backup forces.

"Who can I help?" I announce myself politely.

A gentleman approaches me in an uncommon outfit for Perth city, leather loafers with hidden socks, neatly pressed beige shorts, and a pristine white polo that looks freshly hung and rarely worn. He hands me two luggage tags.

"Just picking up my luggage, please," he says with a grandeur that's also uncommon for Perth city.

"Sure! I'll be back in just one moment," I declare as I swiftly head toward the luggage room.

"Oh, I'll be best to give you a hand. They're heavy," he says, following my movements. It's not uncommon for nice men to offer assistance when they present their bags for collection. We always politely assure them that this isn't our first heavy bag.

"I'm stronger than I look!" I joke with the kind man.

"Oh, no, I mean, these are really heavy." He's now near me at the door of the luggage room. The room is embarrassingly not built for luggage, and is just a storeroom near the front office.

I also don't believe it's a well-built storeroom either. It's often a shambles of buckets or equipment threaded between bags, and it's never in the most orderly fashion. As I unlock the door, I'm disheartened to see that there's not even space to thread myself in to search the numbers on the tags and find the right bag. The gentleman in the polo is now closely behind me as I'm leaning over to read labels.

"It's those two over there," he says closely behind me, startling me. *Is he making me feel uncomfortable, or is it still because I'm a little frazzled by my ill preparation for today's shift?* I thread myself through the bags, hoping nothing sharp catches my stockings, and place my hand on top of his bag. I intend to pull the bag up and over the others, but when I clutch the handle, I realise its sheer weight. I cast a glance over my shoulder to see that the man has begun creating a clear path for the bag, as he knows neither he nor I can lift it over the other bags.

"It's all the crystals," he announces.

I don't take much notice of his comment, as I carefully manoeuvre the bags around the other suitcases and myself. As I get the bags out into the clear path, I look up from my frantic state to see the man staring directly into my eyes. I smile politely.

"Big day for you," he says with a smile in return. *What does he mean by that? Anything happening at the hotel today? Nothing. It's an ordinary day. I forgot my name badge, and I'm now bloody Jessica for the day.*

As I place the last few suitcases back into the room, I think of the mail we received earlier, just before I left for work. A letter of confirmation that Jake is now officially on the Australian donor registry. A month ago, the thought of being on the national list felt worlds away, an impossible achievement. The demands to make the list were hard. Jake had to undergo many steps to be considered. All to prove that he was in fit shape to deserve and receive an organ transplant. Giving up cigarettes was one of the ugliest parts, followed by the several trips to the only bulk billing dentist, scans, appointments, the list felt never-ending for someone who could barely get out of bed. *The lengths they made a sick man go through to get on the list. It really is a big deal.* Only receiving the letter earlier almost seemed insulting. I read the letter, poked my head through the bedroom door and looked at my frail and ill boyfriend. I told him the news and quickly shut the door behind me to allow him to rest.

"I suppose so," I say to the gentleman politely, just to keep the conversation moving.

"Well, at least it's official now," he says as he takes his bags out from under my hands. I stare at him. *What? He has to be talking about the letter. How does he know?* I stare at the man and wonder if I've seen him before. I searched his facial features for any familiarity. Maybe he's a medical practitioner I don't recognise out of his usual uniform?

"Kidneys are pretty important," he says with conviction. Now I search his face harder for where I've met this man. I've stopped moving and being hurried, and I'm just searching his face. As I search harder, the man holds out his hand, as though he's about to formally introduce himself. I'm relieved that he's about to uncover who he is, so I gladly reach for his hand. As I do, the man grabs hold of the outside of my hand; he doesn't clutch it like a common shake, and now he's holding my hand with my palm open and toward the sky. As my palm is facing the ceiling, I begin to connect more dots. There had been a psychic and clairvoyant event this weekend over at the convention centre, which accounts for most of our occupants. This man must have been some kind of psychic, and he does have crystals in his bag. As I realise all of this,

I realise what this man is doing with my hand. He's now staring intently at my palm, and I'm unsure if I want to know what he has to say. My mind begins to race, and I fear the man knows exactly what has been going through my head these past few weeks. *When is he going to die? Will today be the day I come home and he's dead in bed? I think he just needs to die, and I'm ready for that. Life cannot continue as it is; something has to change, and it's his death. Jake needs to die in order for me to continue living.* I begin to worry that my inner thoughts have been exposed, and they are not fit for this world. *They are not fit to be heard by anyone who doesn't understand the hell I'm living.*

"He's going to be okay," the psychic in the polo shirt confirms, as though he immediately answers my biggest question. As the words fall from his lips, I'm unsure if I want that answer.

"Everything is going to be alright. He gets a transplant." The news is so wildly far away from our normal that it's a shock to hear. I feel sick. *The reference point of 'Everything is going to be alright' is so far away! Everything's not alright at the moment. He's not alright. The road between here and everything being alright looks fucking hard.* I'm exhausted just thinking about it. I spiral into thoughts of how anything can get better from here. He needs to be fit and healthy to undergo a transplant. The operation is so extensive that you must be in good enough health to undergo it. The irony being that the only thing that will make him well is a functioning kidney.

"I see... February 12th," he says with a smile and a gentle pat on my hand.

February 12th? This man has now given me a date for his transplant. February 12th. That's four months away. I don't think that's enough time for Jake to get better or fit enough for a transplant.

I begin to put timestamps on these last few months and how long his hospital visits have been, how many times I've traced the brick in our lounge room. The thought paralyses me in the same way the thought 'he'll be alright' does.

The gentleman lets go of my hand and rearranges a few things in his over-the-shoulder man bag. I'm yet to move. Part of me feels indecently exposed. I'm at work, my sanctuary of uniforms, facade and processes, and today hasn't followed protocol in the slightest. I want to start this shift all over again.

"It's okay, Karlee. You're doing really well. Trust yourself." The man in the polo gently pats my arm before taking hold of both suitcases and beginning his journey out of here.

"Can I arrange a taxi for you, sir?" I say, finally finding words and my safe station behind the front desk.

"It's okay, Karlee, I've booked an Uber," he says as he nears the double sliding doors and proceeds out onto the street.

I blankly stare at the computer in front of me, in a quiet lobby, before I'm interrupted by a colleague.

"Um, her name's Jessica," he whispers cheekily.

I struggle once more to find a reply. I stare blankly at my colleague and replay the conversation I just had with the strange psychic. I searched for the part where I'd told him my name. I didn't.

7

I hoped December and the start of summer would bring some warmth to our cold unit, but it hasn't. Somehow, it feels smaller and colder than ever before. Jake is in the hospital, but a new delivery of Icodextrin boxes, his dialysis solution, lines our walls and robs me of space. The boxes, stacked like medical wallpaper, once seemed funny. They don't anymore.

I decide to make a cup of tea. Our small kitchen has never inspired me to cook any nutritious meal before. These plates have mostly held takeaways, and the bowls only cereal.

My hands tremble as I reach for the canister of tea bags and my mug from beneath the kettle. I grip the rough wooden benchtop to settle my hands. *Maybe I'm low on caffeine. Maybe I'm nervous because they haven't been held in quite some time.* As I listen to the kettle gurgle its final bubbles, my phone chimes with a text message. I grab it quickly, in case it's Jake or the hospital calling. Relief washes over me when I see a name from a different lifetime. My oldest childhood friend, Holly.

"K dog! I'm coming to Perth!" I'm immediately warmed. I type back quickly as I watch the three dots dance across the screen, as she types too. I write and write, pour my sore heart out. She doesn't need to hear all that.

Instead, I write: "Ohhh, Holly, that's so good, because I really need a hug." I hit send at the exact moment the phone vibrates with another message from her.

"But sadly, I won't be able to see you!" I read the message, and my chest tightens. I reread the message and watch the three dots dance again as she types. Hopeful in the next message, she's changed her mind. I hold my breath as the dots bounce again. *Surely she'll change her mind. Surely she'll see me.*

My phone chimes, and I read the message eagerly.

"I'm sorry, K. We are travelling south to Margaret River and won't have time to stop." Unsure what to do, I reach for the kettle to pour my tea. The sound of the kettle being placed back in its cradle breaks the silence of my lonely home. I stare blankly at the steam climbing from my mug. I stare at my hands, which once felt the splinters of the rough countertop and now feel nothing. They're numb.

I continue to stare at my hands as they cradle the mug. I sip the tea, but I don't taste anything. No taste. No warmth. *I shouldn't have asked for a hug. I should have just kept a brave front. It's easier that way. Maybe comfort is just something I'm meant to give, not receive.*

♥

Days later, I scroll past all the generic 'Happy Birthday, miss you' messages on Dylan's Facebook wall. *I wonder how many of these people would have sent their birthday messages to Dylan if he were still here?* I read the lengthy posts from his close friends, often accompanied by photos of him and his friends. I imagine the heartache of losing someone so suddenly and without warning. It's hardly the same as what I would experience if I lost Jake. I've been prepared for months. It's as though the hospital is prepared too, as they continuously send Jake home to me, expressing that they can't do anything more than I can at home. Every day for the past week, his dialysis team calls at about ten each morning, which is when Jake is due for his second exchange for the day. They discuss his symptoms, which have been the same for days on end now. I reel them off like a symphony of hell: vomiting, no energy, no appetite and near no urine output. Every day, they request that we present to the hospital via emergency. Every day, we're turned away.

I wonder if losing someone in an accident is any easier than being so prepared for death. *One thing is for sure: dying at this point for Jake would be less painful, and his trip over the rainbow bridge into heaven would be like a well-earned holiday!* I envision his entrance. He'd dance so freely into the place, pulling his dialysis tube from his abdomen and casting it aside. He'd almost immediately greet God and ask for a cigarette. He'd have no luggage, no equipment. I stare with warm and wet eyes at the entrance of our apartment, lined with boxes of dialysis solution.

The stacks of boxes are tucked as closely to the wall as possible and climb as high as safely possible to the ceiling. They are all arranged in their colours, which denote the different treatment strengths: red to green to yellow. I imagine the freedom I, too, would have, leaving those boxes behind, as Jake travels to heaven. I think it is the constant pain and the heavy toll this world has taken on Jake that would make losing him, in some ways, feel easier than losing someone young, fit and healthy in a sudden accident. I centre my focus back to my laptop screen, and back to the birthday wishes that line Dylan's Facebook profile. I remember feeling his death, as I draped Jake's rosary beads around my neck, and I remember the phone call to Chloe the next day. All quite dull and quiet. I begin to type a birthday message of my own for him. I begin with the usual "Happy Birthday, Dylan." *That's a cop out.* I wonder what it is he left behind in this world. I wonder how he'd like to be remembered. I type a few different passages, which all get backspaced. As I continue searching for the right words, I hear Jake on the phone in the next room. Just before 10am, so there's no surprise. He'll be on the phone with his dialysis nurse. I return to searching for the right words to wish Dylan a happy birthday.

As I'm far away in thought, I'm immediately pulled back to the room with a sick stomach when I hear the bedroom door open. As though a ghost has opened the door, because there's no way Jake would be out of bed to do so. He struggled to move unassisted between his bed and the ensuite, clutching walls as he travelled, and never managing to straighten his core at all, always hunched and closer to the ground should he fall. He's not ventured out of the bedroom unassisted for weeks now. I stare in shock as I see his body standing straight. The doorway frames his body in perfect scale, and for the first time in months, I see the complete body of my boyfriend. Not hidden by hospital gowns, or tucked under blankets, or hunched over a toilet or a bucket. His bones hang together by his loose pale skin, and he looks tall, certainly longer than he is anything else. His once-hugging boxer shorts hang loose around his crutch, and it's only his pointy pelvis that holds the elastic waistband on. I stare at his pointed elbow as he holds the phone near his head. I begin to listen to the call, and I don't recognise the voice. I see his every rib expand, just before he finds his words.

"They have a kidney for me," He exhales.

"What?" I respond in total shock.

"They have a kidney for me," He repeats, before he takes hold of the door frame.

I search his unfamiliar body for more answers. Jake holds the phone out toward me, and I immediately find my feet and reach for the phone. As soon as he lets the phone go, his body immediately folds over and gets closer to the ground. Hands stretched out in reach of anything that will support him, he feels for the bed. As I watch him find safety once holding onto the bed, I find the clarity to talk.

"Yes, Hello?" I watch Jake climb back into his usual position in bed.

"Hi Karlee. So, we've got a kidney that's a great match for Jake," his lovely surgeon of Asian descent confirms.

"He's not well, though! He's so sick. We've been trying to get him back into the hospital every day this week," I plead.

"Yes, I'm aware of that," she says calmly.

"But isn't he too sick for the operation?" I look to Jake, who is now curled over on his side, totally in his own world.

"I understand he's sick," she says blankly. "But this is one of the only ways he'll get better."

"So, basically, he'll die if he stays on dialysis?" I bluntly question. The other end of the phone is silent. "Won't he also die on the operating table?"

"Karlee, it's first up to me whether I wish to offer the kidney to Jake, and whether I want to undergo the procedure. I wouldn't have offered this opportunity if I weren't confident that it was a positive move. Or if I didn't think it was for the best…" The doctor catches herself offering too much information before she continues.

"It's entirely up to you. Well, it's entirely up to Jake, and I don't wish to provide any persuasion either way. This is Jake's life."

"Can I ask about how it all came about? What happened to the donor?" I ask in an attempt to take some of the pressure off.

"It was a 45-year-old gentleman, he suffered a head injury at work and never survived his injuries," she says carefully.

"So he died instantly?" I ask without hesitation.

"Well, no, see the thing is…" Our doctor takes a moment to consider her words.

"The donor did survive the accident; he was in ICU for two weeks, before it was concluded he wouldn't survive without assistance. While the impact was to his head, his kidneys never functioned after the accident. This can be…"

"What do you mean?" I interrupt incredulously. "So the kidneys are dead?!"

"It can happen that kidneys go into shock, and that's likely what has happened in this instance," she says smoothly. "With the support of all the other machines, and the inserting of catheters, it can take the need for true function away from the kidneys. They can go to sleep for a while," she says, kindly speaking in layman's terms.

"Well, how do we know they'll wake up? How long until they

wake up?" I question frantically and sceptically. I look at Jake. He's blankly staring at me, his eyes struggling to hold open, expressionless.

"I'm sorry, Karlee, I don't have all the answers. But you need to know that even if you accept this kidney, it will still be me making the call on whether I will transplant the kidney. Once the organs arrive here at the hospital, I will inspect them. I inspect them for their health or any defects, and I'm the one who ultimately decides if I'm happy to transplant them. So, while you have.. Sorry, while you and Jake have a decision to make, you need to be prepared to still be turned away, should I deem the kidney not fit for transplant. However, I'm sorry to rush you, but we don't have time on our side either. This is the third call I've made, and I'll need to make a couple of more calls, depending on your conclusion," she says apologetically.

"Did the first person not take the Kidney? I ask.

"The first match took the first kidney, the second recipient declined." She says blankly.

"Why?" I request instinctually.

"I'm sorry, Karlee, it's not my place to say. Do you and Jake need a little time to think about this? I can give you twenty minutes, but things would need to move quickly after that. You'll need to head into the hospital straight away to begin preparation for surgery, should you decide to go ahead with the transplant."

"Okay. Yes, I have no idea what to do. We'll need a moment to think."

"Okay, not a problem, Karlee, I'll call you back just before 10.30."

As the call ends, Jake untangles his legs from the blankets and begins getting up.

"Are we doing it?" I ask impatiently.

"I don't know. I just need to do dialysis. It's now past ten," he manages painfully.

He begins to make the trip out to the dining table, which is where he performs the exchange when he's well enough to get out of the bedroom. The dining table is always prepared for the treatment. Sterile, clean, and organised. He reaches for a green bag of solution, stacked alongside the chair, and plonks himself on the dining chair with exhaustion. I silently consider our options, and I try hard to visualise whether I can see us in the hospital this afternoon, undergoing the transplant. My mind begins to spiral. *Am I just heading to work like normal in a matter of hours? Or am I about to pack his hospital bag?* I stay quiet as I watch Jake sterilise his hands, before connecting his PD catheter tube to the dialysis bag. We both sigh when we watch the liquid that's been dwelling in his abdomen free itself from Jake's body with urgency and flow.

"What are you thinking, Jake?" I ask urgently. "Do you want to take this kidney?"

"I don't know. I really don't know. What do you think?"

"Babe, I have no idea. I have no idea if it's a good idea. You're sick. The kidney sounds like it's in a bad way. What if it never wakes up? I just don't want to make the wrong decision," I blurt frantically.

"I really just don't know," Jake quietly repeats as he watches the bag filling with his own toxic fluid.

"Jake, it's your life we're talking about here. You need to decide," I plead.

"Babe, I can't. I honestly don't know what to do."

"Right, well, if I said you should take it, are you okay with that? Are you ready to undergo the operation today? You know you're not well. You're not fit for the operation," I begin.

"I know I might die," he bravely interrupts, airing the thought looming over us both.

"Well, yeah. That's the reality of it. This will either be the best decision or the worst decision. I don't think there's any in between," I say bluntly.

Jake looks back down at his dialysis fluid pouring out into the drainage bag. As he does, I suddenly realise the date. *It's December 8th. Dylan's birthday it's not February 12th.* My mind begins spiralling on a new trajectory. *This must not be the kidney we are taking; we must be declining this one and being offered another one in three months' time!*

"Maybe this kidney isn't for us, and we're meant to wait a little longer. After all, someone else has already declined the kidney, too. I wonder if that's because the kidney is in shock and dead, and they're not willing to take that risk. Maybe we shouldn't take it," I reason, pacing the length of our small living room.

"Yeah, maybe. We can wait for another one," Jake agrees.

As soon as he does, I hear how ridiculous it is to be turning down the only thing that will truly fix him. The one thing that isn't readily available. The one thing that requires not only the death of others but a pecking order of who biologically matches them best, weighed up against their cost of life and whether they are more deserving than the person next on the list.

"It's meant to be three to five years waiting for a kidney. We haven't had to wait 3 months! Your doctor basically said it was your only chance," I argue now, as though I'm against Jake's agreement to decline the kidney.

"Okay, we should take it then," he says bravely without hesitation.

His quick change of position frustrates me, and I'm left feeling as though we're no closer to an answer. *We are wasting time!* I take a seat on the couch, and my eyes are immediately drawn to the brick. As soon as I lock eyes with it, I'm reminded of the constant pain and waiting that the brick has helped me through. The lonely nights in the unit, digesting medical terms that I'd picked up that day, and trying to envision our situation getting any better. Trying to envision better times with a healthy boyfriend. The one I knew and had fun with on Long Island. As my mind begins to wander, I urgently check the time.

"Shit! She's going to call any minute, and we don't have an answer!" I announce as I quickly find my feet.

"We don't have to take it," Jake says in defeat.

"What!? Are you sure? It could be another three years on dialysis. And at this rate, you're not going to survive that," I say bluntly.

"Okay, let's take it then," Jake agrees.

As he makes another quick decision, I realise how far away from an answer we truly are. But as I begin to envision the afternoon in the hospital, I remember once more the man in the polo shirt. *He said February 12.*

"Well, maybe we are meant to accept it, but remember it may not happen in the end, if the surgeon doesn't like the look of it. Maybe it won't go ahead, and it won't be our decision."

I pace the room searching for where I left Jake's phone, to ensure we're ready for her call. As I contemplate the phone ringing and us needing to provide an answer, I'm instantly overwhelmed by what we're really deciding here. I look at Jake, ill, depressed, and unable to make a decision about his own health without my input. I stare at the sharp points in his arms and hands and wonder how much of this moment he's actually able to understand. He's only said a few words. None that truly put up a fight for being here. I think about his blank stares at doctors whenever they offer advice. When they diagnose the next harsh fact of our reality. Nothing is new anymore. Every opinion is met with this same blank stare as though this whole episode is a waiting room for a scene that is entirely unfathomable and entirely out of our control. I stare at Jake and wonder if he knows there are only two places on offer today: a room of opportunity or a room that goes nowhere. Today, he needs to walk through one of the doors. Without any idea where to go, he's only listening to my advice and will choose whichever door I tell him to.

"Let's flip a coin," I slightly giggle as I realise what I've said. I'm met with Jake's blank stare.

"I'm serious. Your doctor is calling any second, and I honestly don't have an answer for her. We flip a coin. Because the moment that the coin is in the air, our heart truly makes a choice. If we get an answer we're disappointed in, then we know we want the other option. If we don't disagree with the answer, then we know our hearts content."

I move closer to the dining table in search of my bag and some coins, and take a brief look at Jake. His arm is folded once more as his hand takes hold of his forehead. I find a twenty-cent piece at the bottom of my handbag and move closer to Jake, so he can see me better from his shielded view.

"Are you ready?" I question, demanding his attention.

"Yeah, I guess so," he declares, now looking unwell and ready to return to bed.

"Heads we take it, tails we don't?" I ask. He is silent and returns just a slight nod.

I cast the coin into the air and search that fleeting moment for my heart's answer. *Still nothing.* As the coin drops onto the dining table, I eagerly lean to find the result.

"It's heads. We're doing it," I say firmly. I search Jake's expressionless face for any reaction.

"Are you sad about that?" I ask, peering under his hand to see his eyes.

"No, I don't think I'm sad," he says quietly.

"Okay," I exhale, as I find a dining chair to pull beneath me. The moment I sit down, the phone starts ringing. I stare blankly at the laptop screen in front of me, not really seeing it. Jake answers the phone and informs the doctor of our decision. He speaks as though the decision is informed and well-considered and wasn't made moments ago with the flip of a coin. I remember what I was doing before the call.

"Happy Birthday, Dylan," I murmur. I shut the laptop lid.

8

I step carefully on the uneven footpaths of Sydney's Newtown back streets, just off King Street and close to all of the cuisine and lively characters that live here. I searched for the address to inspect a rental studio apartment. Things have changed a little lately. Jake's health has stabilised (for now) and I can talk to my mum more freely. I've slowly returned to speaking to all those I hid from when my reality was too hard. There's an honesty to my relationships now. No sugar coating how bad things are or how I've been at home scared alone as Jake lay in hospital.

As I try to rush, my legs quickly remind me of how fragile and sore they are. Bringing me back to a cautious pace that won't see me trip on an uneven brick and play out the repeated vision of breaking my hip at a time that isn't convenient. My phone begins to vibrate in my pocket, and I reach for it urgently, expecting it to be Jake, who waits in the hot car on a muggy Sunday in Sydney. It's Mum calling.

"Hey Mum, what's up?" I say quickly, continuing to rush through the narrow streets. I try to listen to mum's pleasantries.

"Listen, I'm just about to go to another inspection. I can't really talk," I interrupt, out of breath.

"I know. That's why I called. Your father and I would like to pay for the rental costs, six months up front. You pay us the weekly rent instead. You need to find somewhere to live and stop spending your days walking around Sydney. You need to get back to university."

I stop mid-stride, the suddenness of her offer catching me off guard. For a moment, I just stand and wonder what to think. Soon enough, the shock is dampened by grim practicality. I'm not sure even that kind of offer will sway a landlord in a city where thirty couples are lined up for a plumbed shoebox.

"Okay, thank you. I'll offer that at the next one. Thanks, Mum, I have to go."

I round the corner and enter a tight one-way street with no street parking, only a single lane and a bike lane. The street is quiet, but I'm immediately wondering where I'll be parking my car. I begin to see several people all walking into the one driveway entrance, and immediately know I've found the unit. I follow the people and form a line. The real estate agent visits each of us in line and asks for our name, marking each of us on her list. I watch as the line disappears quickly. No sooner does a couple enter the unit do they quickly return outside, accepting an application from the agent. As I wait in line, I wonder just how bad this place must be for people to view so quickly.

My phone begins to vibrate again, and I know, by the rough time of day, that it's my alarm to help Jake with another round of dialysis. I hope Jake is awake and comfortable enough in the car to do another round. We've become very good at adapting to our spaces to perform dialysis in the past few weeks while moving from Perth back to Sydney, now carrying an extra dead transplanted kidney. But it doesn't make it any more comforting to know that Jake's sitting in a hot car trying to perform lifesaving treatment.

I watch the man ahead of me in the line thread himself out of the unit and take an application from the agent. I carefully take a step into the unit and realise why people haven't been in there long. There's no space to be in there. A tiny room, which I predict is no bigger than five metres in length and width. With two rooms off to the back, a tiny kitchen, and a tiny bathroom. So small, you need not step inside to see any of the details. Everything is visible in detail from the entrance of the house. It's tiny, but we desperately need somewhere to settle so that I can get back to uni and Jake can try and get better.

♥

As I fold up the pull-out sofa part and build our bed back into our couch, I'm mindful of the time. We really need to head off. There are a few good things about this tiny, cockroach-infested apartment, and one is its proximity to the RPA hospital, where Jake continues to see a kidney specialist.

"Jake, we've got twenty-five minutes to get there!" I shout over the sound of the shower running.

"Yep, coming!" He announces back.

We walk the uneven footpaths at the back of King Street,

Newtown, taking as many shortcuts as possible to the hospital. I'm surprised at how well Jake has kept up, as I set a pace that was somewhat uncomfortable for my fair health. Part of me considers that it's probably due to my decline in fitness, as I carry a lot more weight than when I met Jake. But Jake is now well-versed in this trip, as he travels to the hospital each day for blood tests. At no point does he whinge or comment on the pace. The only comment he makes is to make a joke about having a beer at a pub we were passing. The joke being that this beer-loving man hasn't stomached a beer due to being so unwell for quite some time.

As we near the familiar front of one of the hospitals where this mess began, I acknowledge how much wiser I feel. The old brick building doesn't daunt me nearly as much as it did when I first searched within it for my freshly operated-on boyfriend. We bypass the need to visit the information desk and travel straight up toward the specialist's room. We don't wait long in the chairs outside her room before she calls us in.

We take a seat inside her small office, and as she brings up her files on the computer, I search the aged decor in the room, trying to work out when this room was last given any attention. *It's been decades.*

"Jake, how are you feeling? You're looking much better," she kindly says.

"Yeah, I think I'm doing much better. I haven't needed to do a dialysis exchange in a while now," he informs her, as though her screen hasn't told her that already.

"Yes, that's fantastic. Looking at your results from last week, I'd say we are able to completely say that your new kidney is functioning now. No need for any more dialysis. Congratulations."

The news falls unremarkably on us both. There's no yahooing or celebrations. Just blank expressions. Nothing in Jake's treatment ever goes to plan. And our blank stares express loudly that we're not confident this is it. We're not confident that he is well and that life begins from now. While I have complete faith and confidence in the medical profession and the specialists who have cared for Jake, we have not once had the best scenario. We were promised that our lives would return to normal after Jake started dialysis, yet we experienced far from normal. We experienced a turbulent life, lived hour to hour and full of tension and suffering as we never knew what lay ahead. We experienced isolation as we kept our grim reality locked behind closed doors. Fear and unknowing. Lonely nights, as I'd check the door locks in our cold brick unit while Jake lay elsewhere under cold hospital blankets. Or the nights just after transplant, lying in terror as a steroid-induced rage would take over his body. Countless times staring at three zeros on my phone, acutely aware of exactly what glucose syrup was inside Jake, his exact weight in grams, and every symptom that may trigger a reason to return to the hospital.

Any small procedure always came with an element of risk. And we began to listen to those. The one per cent of side effects that could possibly happen were all presented in waivers before every procedure. I became attuned to reading every point. Reading into the likely reality of the one per cent of things that could go wrong. *Critical haemorrhage, sure. Hypertension, okay. What's a little more blood pressure going to do to him? Sign away. Fever? Well, that's child's play.* There was no waiver that could truly prepare you for how harsh those realities were. Or what the side effects of each of those looked like on a body that couldn't even filter its own toxins. The only way to learn how grim each side effect was was to face it head-on, which we did, time and time again.

While Jake had physically gone through it all, he always seemed to handle everything well. I know that in the worst parts, it was because he really didn't know or understand the starkness of his reality. But I walked every step. Every gruelling step. The armour I had built myself to defend him in an industry not equipped to help any young couple was deeply ingrained in me. While Jake physically faced it, I went to battle every day on his behalf. I kept a roof over our head, I kept our bills paid, I kept the house clean and sterile, free from infection. I called the shots. I would say 'Enough is enough!' and pile us back into the hospital, only to be refused and turned away at my breaking point. I would explain how he was feeling to nurses and doctors. I would question why he'd been discharged only days earlier if they knew about his present symptoms. I put Jake first every day. There was never any help lent to me or my circumstances. A 20-year-old girl, full-time carer, hotel shift worker, and just a month away from completing university…

And now I have a medical professional in front of me trying to tell me that it's all that stops today? Today, it all comes to an end. I struggle to believe that.

Glancing over at Jake, his mind has been elsewhere, digesting the news too. I look back at his specialist, who is still interpreting data on her screen. She realises she's now got our attention back and begins reading a letter to Jake's GP she's prepared while we were off daydreaming.

"Thank you for your continued support of Jake Fowler. His kidney transplant was on December 10th 2015. Jake ceases dialysis treatment today…" She takes a moment from her typing to check today's date on her calendar.

"February 12th 2016."

♥

I completed the last six months of my degree as a completely different student from the free-spirited gypsy who had started it. I'd undergone and juggled a lot with Jake's health and moves and had struggled through all kinds of situations. The last six months in our tiny studio apartment in Newtown saw me work incredibly hard. We were still strapped for cash as Jake remained cooped up inside on the sofa for the whole time. A shadow of whom I fell for years ago. Once confident, sure and the hardest worker in the team, Jake could no longer sell himself to anyone, and struggled to leave the house. I couldn't understand what he was going through, and naturally, my learnt state was to keep fighting for us both. I would rise early and make the quick trip into the city so I could be waiting at the university door for the first staff member to arrive. Regardless of how many classes I'd need to attend that day, I'd set myself up at the same desk in the study area. My friends knew to find me there, and it was one of the few desks that had a good line of sight of the whole room and was conveniently close to a power outlet. I would sit there and work all day, moving only to go to a nearby class before returning. The Woolworths directly underneath our building was convenient for cheap and easy food. I would remain at school until the cleaners kicked me out in the evening, and then I'd head home. Most nights, I would only return home for a short while to say hello to Jake before heading to the local cafe that had Wi-Fi. We hadn't bothered to arrange Wi-Fi at the small studio shoebox, and it hadn't been a problem. I'd get a glass of wine and continue my schoolwork at the cafe until 11pm, before making the short walk home to the unit. Repeating this every day meant I was ahead with most of my university work. I'd discovered that most of my lecturers would accept early submissions of assignments and provide feedback if they were finished two weeks prior to the due date.

Somehow, a girl who'd otherwise worked down to the wire in the years prior, I managed to abuse the privilege. Every assignment came back with sound advice and room for improvement, so I'd spend the last two weeks perfecting the assignment, hand it in with days to spare, no sweat on my brow, and quality work to receive high distinctions. One reason I needed to be so far ahead was that I spent my entire weekends running around a Greek restaurant in Newtown. Just an English backpacker, Aurora, and I were responsible for waitressing the entire restaurant. We had both been unable to get a job anywhere else in Newtown, because, well, to put it plainly, we looked too normal. We were natural girls with no wild hair colour, no sleeve tattoos or piercings covering our faces. We didn't look trendy enough for Newtown.

I worked around the clock for the final six months of my degree, as Jake sat at home in our tiny studio apartment, healing. We had agreed to return to Airlie Beach after I'd finished my degree, as Jake could easily secure a job back on the islands, as he had a good friend up there willing to help us find our feet again. I just needed to get us through these six months of working all weekend and studying all week. Jake was then going to take the reins and let me rest for a while.

♥

Mum and Dad rang with the offer to take me, only me, on holiday to Cambodia as a reward for finishing my degree. A gesture to acknowledge the toll everything had taken and maybe an attempt to reconnect after everything we'd been through. We didn't speak much when Jake had been at his worst, or when I was struggling. They don't want me struggling, but I don't agree with abandoning someone you love in their time of need. The trip feels like an unspoken peace offering, and I'm grateful for it, but I also don't think ten days overseas can undo these knots within me. I've been in survival mode for years now. Years of scraping by to keep both Jake and me alive have etched a deep instinct to keep moving, to keep earning, to never rest. The idea of rest and holidaying feels dangerous when struggle still breathes down my neck.

The day I fly out of Sydney, Jake packs up our little studio apartment, binning the last of the dialysis solution boxes and cramming everything into my car to head north out of Sydney. He is relocating us north, while I begin to unwind and begin my chapter of rest.

The first three days I arrive in Sihanoukville, on the south coast of Cambodia, it downpours monsoonal rain. The first day is manageable as my parents and I joke about not having the desire to do anything other than drink beer and eat good food, which needs no sunshine. However, the constant unclean feeling of being wet and gutter-soaked feet wears thin by the third day.

We have chatted lots, like the old days; however, not once have we spoken a word of what has really unfolded with Jake's health battle and the lengths I've gone to survive the last six months in Sydney. I am enjoying time with my parents, and I feel like a young, reliant child again.

9

We decided to move hotels to be a little more central and have a pool that's readily accessible from our room. We have just gotten comfortable and checked in. Dad heads straight for the pool, Mum starts her laundry ritual of washing her underwear in the bathroom and looking for somewhere to hang them. I plug in our new Wi-Fi details and touch base with Jake.

As soon as I begin to type, I see his green online dot appear.

"How is Airlie Beach treating you?" I ask, picturing him in the town he loves, surrounded by good friends.

"Yeah, fine", he flatly replies.

"So, where are you now exactly?"

"How's your trip with your parents going?" He shoots back.

I try again.

"Where are you now?"

After a pause, he says, "I've been to Airlie, but I didn't feel welcomed. I turned around. Heading south again. I stopped in at Emily's for a bit."

Emily, the ex he came to Australia with. They'd split on Long Island years ago, but stayed good friends. A small island has a way of forcing that. Now she lives with her partner Callum in Agnes Water.

"She and Callum invited us to stay for a while", he continues. "Give us time to figure out our next move."

Just like that, on holidays in Cambodia, I'm now returning to Sydney with no plan, no direction, no job, or job prospects, and barely enough money to look after us for a month. My chapter of rest feels like it's been instantly stripped from beneath me.

Feeling robbed, I end the conversation and make my way out to the pool. The sun has finally made up its mind and appears to have decided to stay. Dad is submerged in the pool with an Angkor beer at his side.
"While you're up, Special!" He jokingly gestures for me to grab him another beer. I make a quick beeline back into our mini bar fridge for another beer.
"Want a beer, Mum?" I yell toward the bathroom.
"No thanks, it's too early! I need a coffee!" She said.

I make my way out to the pool and submerge into this pretty, happier scene, but I'm struggling to find any joy.
"Cheers, Special!" Dad raises his beer to me.
"Yeah! Cheers, Dad," I say with as much mustered energy as

I can find.

"You alright?" Dad's energy quickly shifts to worry.

"Ah, yeah. Just spoke to Jake," I sigh.

"Okay, and Airlie's going alright?" He asks.

"Nope. He's left already. Got up there, didn't feel welcomed, so has turned around for Sydney again."

"Oh, so what's the plan now?" He wonders.

"That's the thing. No plan, no idea of where we can go. No home now. I've got enough money for us to survive about a month. I have no idea what we're going to do." I let out, exhaustion taking over me again. Mum has made her way out to the pool, having heard the last of my worried statement.

"Oh well! Some of the very best times in life come from having no plan. And some of the best opportunities are offered when you've got absolutely nothing else going for you. You should be excited, Special! You're both employable, you've just graduated with a business degree. And, not to mention, you are both well now! It's an exciting time." Dad announces as though he's celebrating this chapter of the unknown.

"Mmm, I guess so. I'm just really exhausted," I declare in defeat.

As my eyes begin to well with the admission, and the weight of the last two years being a primary carer, income earner, decision maker, and genuinely holding our shit together begins to latch onto my chest. I reach for my beer.

"Well, you can always come home…" Mum interrupts. And I immediately feel lighter until she continues with terms. "But we don't open our home to boyfriends."

I sip at my beer and swallow it with tears and fear. No sooner had the armour of tension and constant responsibility loosened ever so slightly as I was holidaying than it took its familiar hold on my chest once more.

♥

Several long, financially scary weeks pass before we finally make it to Emily and Callum's place for a night. Friends from Long Island they've opened their home to us in Agnes Water while we look for work all across Australia. Jake and I both land positions at Heron Island, but it's over before it begins. We arrived by ferry with no one expecting us, and our guts continued screaming 'Run!' for the rest of the day. I was prepared to stick it out and saw the pitfalls as obvious improvements I could make as the appointed Assistant General Manager, but Jake quickly fell apart in a way I'd never witnessed before. Through all his pain and suffering, this was the worst. He pleaded that we leave on the next boat and return to Emily and Callum's to search for something else.

Upon our return to their place, we catch up like months have passed in between. We explain our night away on Heron Island, the poor reception of depressed staff, the slop served in the staff room, the mouldy shacks, and the long journey back across the ocean on the supply barge, as there were no passenger ferries out that day.

"All in all, it was a total shithole!" Jake laughed and brought comedy to the tale, not even slightly indicating how it truly affected him. Once we've explained our eye-opening night away, Emily declares she, too, had some news. All the while I had been writing cover letter after cover letter, and was aware of every vacant position in hospitality around Australia, Emily has actually been in the process of a new job herself. She was letting us in on the news now, as she felt it may soon become a reality. She had one final interview for a hotel manager's position down in Newcastle, where Callum had grown up and had plenty of family. We were excited for her yet wondered why on earth they'd want to leave the town of Agnes Water or the positions they had at the region's leading resort, Seawinds Resort and Spa.

"We can't really climb any further here at Seawinds. Craig's happy and living his dream here. So, I'll need to go elsewhere if I want to one day be a general manager," Emily explained.

"I don't know what I'll do just yet! But I'm happy being a stay-at-home dad, hey Em?" Callum joked, confirming my suspicion that family planning could very well be a driving force behind the move.

"Whatever, Callum. We'll be finding you a job, don't you worry," she teased.

♥

The very next day, just as I was putting off opening the laptop and trawling back through Seek, I received a call from Craig, the general manager of Seawinds Resort & Spa.

"So I'm just about to lose my assistant general manager, and I'm certain I couldn't find a better candidate if I were to advertise, than the young woman who has just graduated from the Blue Mountains International Hotel Management School, who happens to be in town and ready to work!" he says.

Just like that, our situation has gone from dire straits to landing a luxury position at Seawinds Resort & Spa, Agnes

Water, the Gateway to the Southern Great Barrier Reef. Not only have I secured a position, but we have accommodation for as long as we need. Jake, too, will be able to pick up Callum's few days in maintenance, and there are more days available for him in housekeeping. It all seems too good to be true. Our 'normal life' was here: incredible jobs, a roof over our heads, beautiful weather and functioning organs.

10

Five months ago, I picked up a book, 'Miracle Morning' by Hal Elrod. A book that divulges the six habits that will transform your life before 8am. While I may have picked it up and rolled my eyes, I trusted the urge that led me to this book. *I need to transform my life.* I don't think I'd read a book since high school, and I certainly hadn't done any life-changing habits before 8am ever. But I knew something was missing.

Living our days after the kidney transplant, in a version of what we described as 'normal', had become exactly that. We had well and truly found our feet in Agnes Water. I worked hard as a young manager, fostering a team of the very best customer service folk I could scout in this small, sleepy beachside town. And Jake had found his sparkle again. He was embraced by Ezra, the head of maintenance and a fellow Englishman, whose partner (also English), the head of housekeeping, had also been grateful for

THE ART OF ~~LIVING~~ GIVING | 109

Jake's meticulous eye for detail and workmanship. At home, Jake was back to his usual routine of vacuuming beneath my elevated feet, while I tried to relax and repair after almost an entire day standing behind the front desk.

For me, the normal had become quickly mundane. After eight months in my position, I was no longer feeling challenged at work, and physically, I'd become almost unrecognisable. I was the heaviest I'd ever been, and my legs struggled to hold me upright for the day. Mentally, something was missing, too. I didn't know what I longed for or what I felt was missing, but life just didn't feel right.

I hoped this book, which I picked up at Target, would possibly give me direction. *I don't actually expect it to transform my life before 8am, but just a little direction for my life would be great.* After all, I could make myself free before 8am. Nothing was stopping me from getting up early.

The book relied on six habits that needed to be done every morning. It didn't matter how long you spent on each task, so long as you did the six habits every morning. Fondly referred to as the life 'S.A.V.E.R.S,' which stood for Silence, Affirmation, Visualisation, Exercise, Reading and Scribing. I started small, spending just fifteen minutes on the disciplines at the start before I felt it becoming easier to wake earlier. The mornings I'd gone for a walk along the beach to catch sunrise felt as though the day that followed would be lighter. I felt I was awake when the first guest came to check out. And my positive demeanour would reflect in every interaction that followed that day.

Before long, the habit got earlier and continued for longer. I would rise at 5am to ensure I had a chance to sit and have a cup of tea in silence before the day began. I would spend time visualising the best life I could before heading out the door, in darkness, to walk the footpath into Agnes town, and return home along the shoreline as the sun came up. My legs constantly ached. *They've ached for as long as I can remember.* By the time I slipped into my low-heeled hotel professional court shoes for the day, the pain was sharp, but it felt worthwhile. The morning walks lit something in me, and I couldn't wait to do it again the next day.

I found the visualisation step the hardest. *How do you visualise your best life when you believe you're possibly already living it?* I decided that the next book I would read as part of my reading habit should be something to help with this visualisation step. The next book I picked up, the second book I ever read on my own terms, was 'Your Dream Life Starts Here,' by Kristina Karlsson. This was a book on how to discover, chase and achieve your dreams. This book really helped me let go of the limits I wasn't aware I'd put on myself. One of its tasks was to write a list of 101 dreams. I took on the challenge as though it'd be a quick feat. However, the task took weeks and consumed most of my thoughts throughout the day. Each morning, I'd take a new dream into my visualisation and see myself having it.

Two months passed of doing my morning routine, and I'd lost close to fifteen kilos in weight. I had more energy at the end of my days to warrant a beach stroll, and I couldn't wait to wake each morning to enjoy my beach walk. I found it easy to connect with our hotel guests, and thus I enjoyed the satisfaction of seeing many personal dedications to me on the hotel reviews that would appear on Google. One review I received was considerately handwritten and physically signed by a highly successful American businessman, who felt it was important to write to the General Manager of the resort on his return to America about the high service he received from all of the staff members at the resort. He wrote that I needed important recognition as being a cut above the rest. I don't believe I'd changed my style of service or had done anything particularly remarkable to warrant all the compliments. The only thing that had changed was the hour I'd spend on myself each morning before I'd talk to or see anyone else.

Before long, as I sat in silence visualising, I'd seen myself turning up to an open-plan office building in Sydney, commuting to and from a nice apartment in the western suburbs. I'd visualised the business being young, fun, and in a league of its own. One with all the perks included for its employees. While I wasn't searching for just any job, I began researching and looking into the most highly rated companies by their employees, particularly within the travel industry. I found a company called Velari Travel Company that had been newly appointed Outstanding Employer of Choice in a government business award. Out of curiosity, I checked for any open positions. I was captivated by the only role available in their Sydney office, which was for an Office Manager position within their human resources team. The position played a large part in the onboarding of new employees and maintaining a positive company culture. I prepared and applied for the role before I'd even mentioned to Jake that I dreamed of being in a company culture in Sydney.

As the weeks passed, the vision of working in that role became stronger. Each morning, I'd wake in the sleepy town of Agnes and spend ten minutes with my eyes shut, commuting to my role at Velari Travel Company. I hadn't heard anything back after my application, which rather suited the fact that I also hadn't told Jake I'd been visualising a life far from this town, a town he was loving. To assist my visualisation, I felt it was important to follow up about my application, so I knew if it was time to move on to a new dream or not. I upgraded my LinkedIn subscription to premium, so I could personally reach out to the employment team at Velari Travel Company. I sent a kind message stating how I'd come across the company and why I wanted to be aligned with a company that valued its people. I mentioned that it would be nice to know if I'd been successful or not in the application process, as I wasn't looking for any other job.

The following day, I received a phone call from the head of HR, Ashleigh. She asked about the possibility of meeting me for an interview. As luck would have it, I was heading to Sydney that weekend to catch up with some friends from university, so I proposed meeting with them in person on Friday; otherwise, it would have to be a phone interview. Ashleigh jumped at the chance to meet me in person, and just like that, I'd secured an interview for two days away, meeting Australia's outstanding employer of choice, Velari Travel Company.

♥

The office where I met with the company's founder and HR team was far more beautiful than I had imagined. There were tiny details that I had missed in refining my vision, like the regal blue carpet that melted underfoot and the freshly cracked San

Pellegrino sparkling water atop the marble coasters. My capability to do the role also felt a better fit than I had imagined. The interview went smoother than I had envisioned, too. I spoke of how important a good team culture was to me, and how I fostered meaningful relationships with my existing team. I left the interview feeling prouder of myself than ever before, for the leader, employee, manager, and young lady I had become both professionally and personally.

Just as I neared the pub that afternoon, where I would meet my friends from university, my phone began to ring. It was Ashleigh. Just two hours after I'd left the interview, and I knew instantly that it was either going to be a sure-fire 'Yes', or a polite 'No'. Ash cut straight to the chase, requesting I submit my notice of resignation to Seawinds Resort & Spa today, so I could commence in exactly 4 weeks' time, a week prior to the company's large 15th birthday celebration, which would need my assistance to pull off.

I awaited the arrival of my friends before I suggested a bottle of bubbles, demanding they celebrate with me. We all got settled, and I announced my news as glasses clinked. I sipped the champagne in the presence of friends I'd missed and forcingly swallowed. I realised now it was going to be really hard to tell Jake the news.

♥

The six morning disciplines continued after moving to Sydney, and before long, they seemed to be more important and sacred than ever before. I continued the habit in the wee hours of the morning, and now living in a city, this hour felt even more silent, as though it held a secret that very few would ever stop to appreciate. The alarm was set at 4.30am, and I'd slip out from our bedroom without disturbing Jake. I would spend the first forty to fifty minutes dedicating my time to silence, affirmations, visualisation, reading and scribing. Then, just as I'd hear Jake snooze his alarm from the bedroom, I was out the door for exercise. I would hit the same local walking track that took me just under an hour to complete, often meaning I'd return home after Jake had left for work.

As the routine continued for months, I had one vision that occupied my thoughts most mornings and continued to weave through my mind when I'd be on my walk and followed me into the rest of my working day. It had stemmed from a few dreams listed alongside one another on my list of 101 dreams. The vision entailed a man returning home from work, leaning over, and embracing two excited kids. At the front door of an earthy brick home, I sensed my own delight for his return and the feeling of calm and laughter he brought home with him. The vision played over and over. Each time I struggled to make out more of the surroundings, I could never see his face. Each time I looked toward the man's face, something would mask his features. The vision replayed for months on end, and with every attempt at seeing the man's face, I'd come to realise why I couldn't make out the face. I didn't know who it was, but I knew it wasn't Jake.

I continued the routine each morning, and much like the vision of the job in Sydney, the same details repeated as though there was no room for anything else. No matter how hard I tried to envision any other dream, all that occupied my thoughts was this vision of a family that didn't include Jake. What was hard to imagine was my reality without Jake. We had become so intertwined over the years, and had gotten to know each other in each version we'd become. I knew Jake as confident, I knew him as sick, I knew him when he was comfortable, and I knew him when he was unhappy. He hated leaving Agnes Water and moving back down to Sydney. And I hated being around someone so miserable. After everything he had been through, he just wanted his life to return to how it was pre-transplant: days of working hard by the beach, and rewarding himself each night with beers. It was a stark contrast to all that had changed for me. I couldn't help but feel as though while he got the new organ, I got the new life. A chance to create a better, healthier life, with all the lessons I'd learnt juggling everything over the years. The patience and grit that I'd uncovered within could be used wisely. I knew I could utilise my communication skills, emotional intelligence, and grit to achieve whatever I wanted. I just couldn't go anywhere yet, as Jake and I had a trip to the UK booked so that Jake could be his brother's best man at his wedding.

♥

As I peer through the window of the Uber, I scan for the house number. Then I see it. A dark bricked terrace house, with almost gothic-like trims strung together with cobwebs. A faded green door with the number 18 barely clings to the wood. This is it.

I thank the driver and slide out of the car. As I near the door, a strange wave of recognition washes over me. This is the house. It's the same house I've been seeing in my morning visualisations. The same green door, its faded number, the cracked step leading up. I'd never seen more than a front door, but it was always this door.

I hadn't been visualising it for long. Maybe just two weeks since we returned from our overseas trip. The breakup was already in motion by then. I'd brought it up in Italy, after another evening where I devoured sourdough dipped in olive oil and mature balsamic, while Jake ordered a pepperoni pizza and spent the whole meal tearing it apart with complaints. We were two different people, and it wasn't just our taste in food. It was about joy. I was searching for it everywhere. He couldn't see it anywhere.

And what hurt more, what left behind a dull ache, is that I paid for the entire trip. I even funded for his mum and brother to join us for a week in Italy, thinking it would be a rare and special time to share. But they, too, spent most of their time complaining. About the heat, the walking, and the food. Everything. I gave everything I could, and it still wasn't enough. It didn't just hurt me. It changed something in me. It made me realise I was pouring from a cup that had long since dried up. I knew I had to say something before we returned home, in case he wanted to return home to England. I wasn't sure he'd cope in Sydney without me, but to my surprise, he wanted to stay in Australia. He wanted to return to our apartment in Canterbury, where we lived with Ben, one of my closest uni friends.

Ben had given me his blessing to move out, told me not to worry about him living there with Jake. And just like that, after all we'd been through, Jake and I hugged goodbye through tears and agreed to let go completely. No contact. No friendship. Nothing left between us but the shared years. The big, full years.

And now, I'm standing at the door I didn't know existed, yet somehow already recognised. Ready for whatever was behind it. Ready for the next chapter.

11

I settled into my Pyrmont home. It was just as homey and as perfect as the vision had suggested. My morning ritual had softened. It was no longer a survival mechanism, but rather an aid for dreaming. I began visualising myself in a new role at work, one I felt was out of reach. Just weeks later, the exact position unexpectedly opened, and I was encouraged to apply. It felt surreal. *Another morning vision has become my reality.*

The exercise component had been a particularly challenging element of the morning routine to maintain. My niggling left hip, which had been quietly keeping me slower than most people my whole life, had become a louder pain. And while I tried to visualise my way out of the pain, it never worked. It was as though it got louder each time I stepped more fully into myself. For instance, when I transitioned to a new career in Sydney, or when I finally chose myself over the relationship. *It's like the momentum stirs it up, but the pain wants me to stay still.*

Just like everything else in my life, I knew it needed more conscious effort. To find a fix or at least investigate why it is as bad as it is. I knew the basics. I was born with a disorder that ran sporadically in our family: Multiple Epiphyseal Dysplasia. It's led to early hip replacements, and my cousin Wayne had great results with some early reconstructive surgery. I started to wonder if maybe that could help me, too.

After doing my research on some leading hip specialists, organising the necessary scans and some referrals, I landed in Dr. Mi's office.

I glanced around the office, still catching my breath after the whirlwind dance of physical examinations. He's blunt and quick-moving as though he knows the answers already. With no conversation, he sits across from me at his desk, eyes fixed on his computer. He adjusts the mic that's attached to his monitor, then speaks.

"I have explained to Karlee that in view of her degenerative changes, comma, there is absolutely no point in considering any form of conservative hip surgery, full stop." He quickly makes eye contact with me before returning his eyes to the computer.

What? He's not explained anything to me!

Now convincingly resembling a mad professor, he launches into a rapid-fire explanation of the formation of my hip joint. Full of technical terms, not suited for a patient's understanding. Then continues to dictate.

"In the end comma, a hip replacement is the only effective solution full stop. The timing of surgery is a quality-of-life decision full stop. In the interim comma, strengthening hip abductor musculature as well as losing a couple of kilograms will help with pain relief full stop."

Great. So, my hip hurts because I'm fat.
I hold my gaze firm, trying to mask the pain of his final line. I watch as he fiddles with the mouse and keyboard, clicks the end of his pen, clangs it back into the pen holder, then folds his hands together, turning to me with a smile.

I climb to my feet and head for the door before he gets any chance to say another word.

I've never felt smaller while being convincingly told I'm too big. *Too fat. So fat that my hips are hurting.* And yet, they hurt now, even after losing weight. *I'm trying.* I'm trying to look after myself. *But now I wonder: what's the point? Maybe I'm really just better at looking after others.*

♥

It's early January, my first day back after the Christmas break, but the new year doesn't feel fresh. It feels stale, like a continuation of a strange chapter I don't want to be in. Six months since the breakup, four months into my new role as partnerships specialist, and instead of feeling motivated to plan upcoming events, I'm reading another message in the family group chat about who can help Brendan move his cows today.

The pit of discomfort digs deeper as I sit in the eerily quiet Velari Travel Company office. It's not the productive kind of quiet. It's the tense, fearful kind where no one dares breathe too loudly. Sienna, our once energetic head of Marketing, has shifted tone dramatically. She's been holding strange one-on-one catch-ups and just yesterday fired the travel writer out of nowhere. Something has changed.

And at home, in Woodleigh, things have changed too. Two days after Christmas, my eldest brother, Brendan, had a farming accident, which resulted in him being pinned under a trailer full of hay bales. For days, while we waited for results, we didn't know if he'd walk again. I'd never paid attention to ramps and disabled parking before those days in limbo. But I began to see them everywhere. Wondering how life might change for my brother. Thankfully, the verdict came back: broken vertebrae and no permanent damage. Still, he couldn't work his farm without help. My parents and my other brother, Billy, were stepping in. I couldn't. Not from Sydney. Not from this suffocating desk.

My life in Sydney felt selfish by comparison. I travel often for events in Australia's major cities, staying out late at partnership functions that fed me dinner and wine before I'd stroll fifteen minutes through Darling Harbour, over Pyrmont Bridge, to my converted attic on the top floor of my dream townhouse. It was a good life, but at this moment, it feels disconnected.

While I enjoyed the partnerships specialist role, working with major tourism boards to build campaigns. There were parts that never sat right. Unlike my manager and many of the marketing team, I didn't spend my pay cheque on clothes or my mornings on elaborate hair and makeup routines. My own morning routine was what attracted the wonderful things in my life, not the labels I wore to work. The difference in values is subtle, but it was always there.

"Karlee, can I see you in the boardroom?" Sienna asks.

Her tone is sharp and falsely sweet. I follow her in, sit across the table, and for the next forty-five minutes, she dismantles me. Not my work, me. Everything that makes me, me. My attitude, my relationships with partners, my relationships with my colleagues, everything that makes me likable. It's as though she finds anything worth complimenting me about and turns them into blunt criticisms. Her message is clear: I need to dull my sparkle.

By the time I step back into the office, I've made my mind up. I gather my laptop, company credit card, work phone, and anything else that ties me here. I walk straight over to my old department, and the team who know me most, HR.

"Sorry, girls, I'm done," I say, setting the pile of belongings down on their desk. The three girls stare at me, startled. "Wait… What do you mean?" The kind women all rise to their feet.

"She's flicked her switch on me too." I make subtle references to other abrupt departures from her team in the past.

"Karlee, wait. We can move you into another department. You don't have to work with her."

"No," I simply say. "I can't work here anymore. Not after this."

My lovely old team bargain again, but I'm already gone in my head. My brother isn't well. Life is precious. No one's life depends on me staying here.

Just minutes later, I'm on the footpath outside the building.

It's all over. Every inch of my body feels uncertain. *Am I trembling with fear? Or jittering with excitement?* I'm lighter without the load of all the devices and keys that had crowned me as one of the most trusted employees. My two feet, in practical flats, not a piercing stiletto, hold my orthotics and support my free and trembling next steps. My phone buzzes in my pocket. It's Celeste, my ex-manager of ten minutes ago. I let it ring out. I feel my phone buzz again and half-heartedly glance at the screen, ready to ignore the calls once more. This time, it's a number that's not saved, and curiosity gets the best of me.

"Hello?" I carefully answer.

"Well, hello, Miss Hayes!" An easily identifiable Portuguese Mafa fills the other line.

"What?! Hello Mafush! How are you? Where are you?" I ask.

"I've just landed back in Australia, Miss Hayes! What are you up to?" she asks curiously.

"Well, nothing! Absolutely nothing. I just walked out of my job and I'm literally standing out the front of my office building, wondering what the hell to do with my life now!" The bubbling excitement and fear fill every word that comes out of my mouth.

"Oh wow! Well, that suits me perfectly! Save me the story and let's catch up for a beer, ay!" Mafa promotes humorously, yet seriously.

"You know what. That sounds perfect. Have you literally just landed, or are you in the city?" I wonder how soon she's referring to.

"I'm in the taxi heading for Bondi, but how about we meet at The Bells hotel in Woolloomooloo?"

"That sounds great. I'll walk that direction now and will be there in about twenty minutes."

"Perfect, Miss Hayes. See you then!"

12

I tried to make South Gippsland, Victoria, where I grew up, feel like home again. After walking away from my job in Sydney, I returned to Victoria so I could be closer to my family. I was able to help Brendan as he healed. However, while little had changed at home, I had. I'd grown in ways that made the place feel smaller and colder, just not quite right for me anymore. Something about it also made me feel like I was taking backwards steps. And I really needed forward motion. I needed momentum.

I began searching for live-in roles across Australia, something to take me somewhere new. I was looking at hospitality roles, my profession, such as Live-in manager and resort roles, that sort of thing. But I stumbled on something much more meaningful. An ad that pulled at something far deeper within me.

A live-in carer/nanny role supporting a mother living with a disability, her husband who works away and their three children. I had no formal qualifications to suit, but I had plenty of lived experience, enough to demonstrate I had what it took to care for someone completely.

I wrote a heartfelt cover letter and hit send. Twenty minutes later, Anna, the woman from the ad, phoned me and offered me the job on the spot. I packed my beloved Honda CR-V again and drove north to the suburb of Kenmore, on the outskirts of Brisbane. And now I'm here.

"Just breathe. It's a lot to take in, I know," says Roxy, the woman who's been left to train me in my new role. She stands at the door of the laundry and waits for me to tighten the lid of the soaking urine bottle. I take one last glance at the sink, hoping my visual memory will cement the routine Roxy just taught me in just fifteen seconds. I follow her out the door.

"Now, we'll quickly throw some vegetables in the oven for Anna's dinner," she says briskly, walking toward the kitchen. "Then we'll go back and check on her in the shower."
The quick change in tasks makes my sweaty head feel hotter as I struggle to keep up with the wise woman in Brisbane's humidity.
"So, where in Victoria are you from?" Roxy asks as she rifles through the fridge crisper.
"Oh well, originally from Victoria, but I've lived all over the country these last couple of years." I breathe a little easier as I feel for the first time today, I could do something with ease; talk.

Our conversation over chopping vegetables is interrupted by a faint banging sound.
"Oh! That's Anna, she's ready for us!" Roxy says, dropping the knife and immediately heading down the hall toward the

bathroom. As she passes the hallway cupboard, I witness a thought come across her quickly moving body. She quickly stops and opens the cupboard door. Her hand intentionally reaches for one pile within the cupboard and pulls out a small aqua hand towel. She passes it to me with a smile and says considerately, "She's always cold. It'll be very hot in the bathroom, so you might want to use that for your brow!"

We enter the bathroom, and Anna has her arms folded across her chest, clutching the handheld shower head as it washes water over her seated belly. I can tell we startle her from thought, and immediately she verbalises her thinking.

"So, did Jake ever try any natural healing remedies when he got sick?" She asks as I find a spot to stand out of Roxy's way in the bathroom. I watch Roxy as she sanitises her hands once again, then reaches for one face washer that's propped strategically along a fixed handrail. Roxy's eyes meet mine, and with just a glance of her eyes on mine, I know I need to pay close attention to this next part.

"Ahh, things were pretty serious from the moment he was sick, so there wasn't a lot of space or time for natural remedies," I explain as I watch Roxy habitually reach over Anna's shoulder, holding the washer out for her to wet with the shower head. Her mind ticks as she continues to consider my response.

"Well, there's always space and time for natural remedies. There's a lot more than just Western medicine that the body can use to heal," Anna sternly confirms as Roxy continues to lather the washer with exactly one and a half pumps of soap from the white dispenser, she pointed out to me.

"Yeah, of course there is," I nervously agree in fear of continuing the discussion of natural remedies in a life-or-death situation.

"So, just with a soft open hand, we're just going to reach

underneath Anna and get the spots she can't reach." Roxy meets my eyes and strategically disrupts the conversation. "So, we just want to do a good wipe across both cheeks, and any part of the thighs that are creeping through the shower chair, then with a soft karate style hand, just one wipe from the front of her bits to the back. Easy!" Roxy respectful explains with a smile on her face, as I return one to her in the hope she can't sense my discomfort.

"Then, we'll steal that shower head off her and give her a rinse down from our spot back here!" Roxy explains with ease and enthusiasm.

"Then, when Anna's ready, she will turn off the shower, and we'll quickly get her a towel, so she doesn't get cold."

In a few swift movements, I watch Roxy wheel Anna out from the shower, into the centre of the room beneath the glowing heat lamps. She shows me two towels that are draped behind the door. Making a point, she grabs the pink towel and drapes it across Anna's front. Roxy takes the white towel and positions herself ever so carefully within a small gap that's between the back of the shower chair and the basin sink. She ensures I take note of the basin and how closely the chair is positioned. As though to explain without words, that for one reason or another, the chair should be exactly there, and you'll need to be careful of what follows.

I watch as Roxy drapes the long towel carefully across her forearm and over her hand, as she then crouches down in the small space.

"Now, just as we did in the shower, we'll dry Anna's underside. But be careful not to let any part of any towel touch the floor." Roxy briefly states, her voice carrying a warning she's clearly heard before.

"This room is where a lot of Anna's personal care happens, so everything has to be kept as clean as possible. If a towel brushes the floor, we'll need to get a fresh one, because even a tiny bit of bacteria could put her at risk of an infection."

"So, it's best just not to let the towel touch the ground, okay?" She questions with a smile on her face, as though I shouldn't be concerned. I understand there and then I'll never allow that towel to touch the floor. It wasn't just a rule; it was her safety, and part of the invisible weight of responsibility that she now trusted me with.

♥

Two months have slipped by, and not dropping the towel has already threaded itself into the long list of things I did without thinking, and as though my job depended on it.

"I just turned the pot down for you," I politely interject as Tayla walks hurriedly toward the back door, clutching the full washing basket upon her hip. Her eyes, which were scanning the room for the bird of the house, our resident feathered escape artist, began to look for me.

I straighten myself from my slouched position as I scroll through Instagram while eating breakfast.
"Oh! Thank you!" Tayla's face lightens, and I watch her brow uncurl into a smile as she makes proper eye contact with me. "Good morning! How are you?" She relaxes ever so slightly to ask me.

"I'm all good." I dust my fingers free of toast crumbs and turn properly toward her. "What about you? Going okay?" I ask softly, knowing by the untidy kitchen and an additional full washing basket sitting at the back door needing to be hung out, that the shift must not be going in her favour.

"Yep, good." Tayla bravely nods and swallows, forcing a smile before searching for her words. "What about you?" She asks again, shifting the weighty washing basket of sheets to her other hip as she tries to hide her urgency to get out the back to hang them.

I could laugh. I shouldn't laugh. She's already asked me. Poor girl. Glad I'm not the only one who struggles.

"I'm all good, darl. You get those out. I'll do the other basket for you," I say with a little nod to free her from the distracting chit chat.

I watch her shoulders drop inches as she lets go of some of her tension. Just as she starts to form a thank you on her lips, a cry for her is heard. Tayla's eyes instantly look to the sky. A plea for a break. She lets go of her breath and places the full washing basket by the other one at the door.

Her brow lifts as she pulls a forced smile and heads toward the cry. Her quick steps break the silence. "On my way!" she calls out, casting one final look my way.

Her anxiety lingers in the air behind her. I feel it too. The ache of never being able to finish one task before the next pulls you away.

And it's not only Tayla.

As I make my way back into the house after my morning routine, I peek at the kitchen bench to see which of our team's belongings are there. I can see by the Keep Cup and phone that it's Marley, one of the younger carers. She's one of the efficient ones. Sometimes, it felt as though some of the carers left behind a lot of household chores for me because I lived there. While I understood their view on that, it often meant that my day, already full of the household routine, became a bit heavier. Or on a day off, like today, Marley rarely left any stone unturned, and if ever she did, she would have made all attempts for that load to be as light as possible on me.

At the sight of Marley's belongings on the bench, I knew I could shower, then head to the kitchen and make my breakfast without needing to clean a sink load of dishes or create space in the kitchen. There was minimal destruction in the kitchen when Marley was on shift, and she very rarely left any dishes for me to clean throughout the day.

I opened the door to my bedroom and got a whiff of something burning. I quickly dumped my sweaty gym towel in my ensuite and headed toward the kitchen, and the smell. I checked the oven and could just make out some very dark orange squares, either pumpkin or sweet potato, now long beyond anyone's tolerable degree of cooking. I turned off the oven and pulled out the tray, carefully placing it atop a wooden board. As I pondered my next moves, I heard the hallway cupboard open and knew I could quietly call for Marley's attention.

"Morning, Marley!" I sing out.

"Oh! Morning Karlee!" Marley politely shifted her attention from the towels she was putting away and moved closer to the kitchen. "Oh shit!" she cries, spotting the tray of burnt food.

Marley briskly puts the towels away and quickly makes her way to the kitchen.

"Ah, damn it!" she says.

I sense her defeat and immediate assessment of how much time she has to achieve all her tasks. Her calculations continue to defeat her.

"I'll put some more on for you?" I suggest.

"No, no, it's okay. I don't think I'll have enough time," she says, tapping at her phone to check the time. "Ah, I'll just have to tell her she's not having sweet potatoes today," she sighs defeatedly.

"Hmm, we could give it a little head start in the microwave and then into the oven?" I suggest in an urge to help. As I do, I realise Marley is hesitant at the mention of the microwave.

"I know she doesn't like us microwaving much... but it would speed it all up," I try to convince and assure her. Marley's whole body begins to slump, yet she maintains her speed and sense of urgency. She scrapes the tray's burnt contents into the bin as I search for more ways to fix this situation.

"We can cut them into even smaller squares, so they cook even quicker!" I propose, in a real attempt to fix this. As I do, I realise Marley won't be keen on that option either, as no doubt she too would have been critiqued over the size of the squares that Anna likes her vegetables cut. I search the veggie crisper for another sweet potato. Looking up at Marley, our eyes meet as she realises she used the last of the sweet potato. Somehow, now, she looks even more defeated by the whole ordeal.

"I've got time to race down to Coles and grab another?!" I cry quickly, desperate to help her fix this mess.

I watch Marley reach for her takeaway cup and calmly take a sip. I'm not sure if I see the last ripple of defeat or cold coffee crawl her skin as she lets out another sigh. "She's just going to have to go without sweet potato today. It's not the end of the world." Marley says, trying to comfort herself.

"She won't die!" she concludes finally.

We share a look across the kitchen, heavier than words. It isn't just burnt food she's grappling with. It's the mental weight of having failed at another task.

And I realise: It's not just Tayla with her arms aching, or Marley with her mind racing. Here we all struggle together. Always longing to meet every demand, to meet every need perfectly, to keep pace with the demands, to anticipate without ever falling short. But it is a rhythm no one can sustain, and no mind can master. The struggle is constant, carried collectively, and the ache is always the same. It's the ache of knowing that no matter how hard we try, it can never quite be enough.

♥

After waking with a headache once again, the morning routine is pushed to the side. I lie freshly showered and dressed on top of my made bed and quietly attempt to motivate myself for the day. So does Kia, the family cockatiel, who's out of her cage, squeaking for attention on my lamp. Filled with sass, yet is somehow very lovable for someone who's never known or liked birds. Why do I like you again? I glance sideways at her.

I know the moment I walk through the door into the living room, I'll be quite likely needing to drag Maddie and Ava around the house to try and get them ready for netball. *I hope they're at least fed and have their patient listening ears on this morning.* Their little brains handle a lot of emotions before 9am in this house.

Maddie is 12, sharp and witty. She's a daddy's girl, obsessed with her switch and always decked out in whatever brand is trending that week. Ava, on the other hand, is a quintessential eight-year-old girl, equal parts sweet and dramatic, who loves pink, anything fluffy, and will perform a pirouette mid-sentence.

As I wonder how they might tackle the morning, I hear a gentle knock at my door.

"Karls! Can we come and brush our teeth in your bathroom?" Ava's innocent voice calls through the door.

Delighted that they're willingly brushing their teeth, I spring from my moment of prayer-like state and eagerly open my bedroom door.

"Well, of course you can!" Swinging the door open, I greet both Maddie and Ava with a big smile. I watch as Maddie's face washes over with a smile, even as she tries to control it.

"Good morning, my little friends!" I tease, grabbing them both into a rough and playful cuddle.

I assess the entire productivity of the morning purely based on Ava's brushed hair, Maddie being dressed, including socks, and the absence of their breakfast dishes on top of the loungeroom's coffee table. I predict that with Maddie and Ava's cooperation, Leah is home from uni this morning, helping out. She works well with the kids, and they always listen to her.

Maddie and Ava follow me into my ensuite. I grab my

toothbrush too, and offer them my toothpaste. Ava lights up, staring at me in the reflection of the mirror.

"Are you going to brush your teeth too?" she enquires excitedly.

"Yep! Of course. You can't leave the house without brushing your teeth," I assure her, swinging the toothbrush into my mouth. All three of us stare back at each other in the vanity mirror.

"Well, you actually can," Maddie pauses her brushing to sarcastically state.

Ava and I both roll our eyes in unison, which makes us both burst into laughter. Simultaneously, we frantically move our free hand to our face to catch the toothpaste that falls from our mouth. The sight of us both makes Maddie begin to laugh too, and before we know it, we're all spitting our toothpaste into the bowl to save a larger clean-up.

"Karleee!" Ava screams in playful blame that I caused all of this mess.

"Ayy! That was Maddie!" I point my toothbrush, flinging toothpaste in her direction. Maddie drops her jaw in shock, then lets go of a big laugh.

"Well, you actually can!" I mimic her earlier remark.

Maddie and Ava both continue to laugh and embrace the mess that's happening around them. They are genuinely carefree, and as happy as I've ever seen them. I can't help but get carried away in their childlike play. *My favourite part of my job.*

As we continue to brush our teeth, I bask in the rarity of us all sharing in the same emotion. *All they really want is for their life to be shared.* From play to good habits, these two miss sharing moments with their parents. Over the last eight months, I'd made numerous attempts to have their mum or dad share moments with them. I'd insist on picking their mum up out of her chair and putting her onto the couch with one of them under each of her arms when we watch a movie together.

As we brush our teeth and share sideways looks, I realise their true frustration. When I first started in this role, I thought these kids didn't understand how difficult it was for their mum to be in a wheelchair, and Dad needing to work away, but now I know that, of all people, they understand it most. They're most frustrated by all the times they watch their parents choose routines, therapies or responsibilities over them. *They really don't need much at all.* After all, we'd just shared the most heartwarming moment, simply brushing our teeth together. Something their mum is doing right now, just in another room.

♥

"Where were you?" Anna asks me later that day, as soon as I step into the bathroom.

"Sorry. I had to get the sheets off the line," I reply as my mind immediately thinks of ways I could lift her mood or change the subject.

"I found some flipping perfect pears today at Coles!" I comically sing as I lather the face washer for her evening routine.

"Oh, did we need more pears?" she asks in shock.

"Well, you've got some hard green ones ripening on the bench. But they're a few days away," I explain, crouching down to clean her underside.

"Urgh, no one thinks when they do the shopping," she bluntly swipes.

"Well, you've now got some ripe pears for the morning!"

I positively confirm.

"We'll need to wash my hair tonight, honey," Anna announces as I rinse her down.

"Oh, okay, sure," I agree, hiding the weight that this adds to my load for the evening. "Well, I best go turn the oven down now if so," I suggest, as I reprioritise the list of tasks that need to be done.

"Can't we eat dinner together first, then you can dry my hair just before bed?" she suggests.

"Sure!" I say, as I resign myself to missing the chance to eat my dinner alone. Also, meaning the dishes and the entire kitchen/house tidy-up will now fall to the very bottom of my to-do list for the evening. If it doesn't get done tonight, then the load will only pile tomorrow. It's a full-time job in itself to keep this house to Anna's standard. *It's a standard I share. I just can't relate to all the other things she prioritises.* All needed to somehow be done in record time and as quietly as possible, so Anna could get to sleep. Only then will I finally retreat to my bedroom and wind down for the day.

♥

If it isn't hard enough to juggle the daily load of caring for Anna, her kids, and myself, I've pushed myself further and signed up for '75 Hard', a mindset challenge that requires daily disciplines without exception. Every day, you must honestly and completely drink four litres of water, complete two workouts (one outdoors), take a progress photo, follow a meal plan, no alcohol or cheat meals for seventy-five days straight.

I figure it's a way to get back into my old morning routine, as many of the elements crossed over. *Any improvement in my health is welcome right now. I haven't quite felt myself lately.*

The challenge is working. I really am mentally tough. My head feels clear and sharp. I wake early and leave just as the morning shift arrives, so I don't wake Anna with the opening of the loud front door. I drive to the gym and park. Then, depending on how my hips feel, I either walk or run around the nearby lake before heading to the gym for a strength session. That's half the daily disciplines finished before 10am.

Balancing the rest alongside work with Anna isn't easy, but I find ways. The discipline itself seems to fuel me. The structure, the movement, the small wins. I need it all because my days are full. There's always a constant stream of washing *(she likes fresh sheets daily)*, twice daily showers, meal prep, daily juicing, cleaning the juicer, handwashing dishes, managing supplements, sourcing ripe pears, picking up after the kids, ironing the clothes they've dragged out, and all the other details that fill the house. The days roll one into the next, and a clear head helps me juggle it all.

The tricky part is my days off, when I finally get the chance to relax and catch my breath. They've become more exciting since I met Noah online. A tall, blonde-haired and blue-eyed handsome surfer, whom I couldn't have swiped right on faster. I wasn't really searching for a relationship. I was bored and lonely one afternoon, and I thought it might be fun to chat with someone. It was fun chatting to Noah, and that translated into real life when we caught up in person.

I felt confident in my own skin, not needing the date to be

anything more than enjoyable, so I decided to show up as my true self. Embracing all flaws. No makeup. A singlet that revealed my arms and shoulders. And it all went in my favour. We got on well, although in person, Noah was much taller and more reserved than I expected. I drive down to the Gold Coast to spend my days off with him, only I have weekdays off, and he works the usual tradie schedule. That usually means we only get to spend the afternoons together.

"Yum! Thanks, K Pop," Noah says, accepting the Tupperware container I'd prepared for our picnic date so we could hang out while I stick to my meal plan.

"You're welcome! Extra chicken and chilli in yours, sir!" I say, pulling up alongside him on the sand.

"So how was your week with the crazy lady?" He asks with a cheeky grin, his tone more teasing than cruel.

"What? She's not crazy!" I shoot back, instantly defensive. "I've never called her that!" I eat a mouthful of rice, unsure of what to say next.

"Relax," he chuckles. " I don't mean it like that. It just sounds like a lot sometimes."

He's right. But how does he know? I always consciously defend her, not knowing what I'd be like if I became wheelchair bound.

"You'll tell me something ridiculous you had to do," Noah continues through a mouthful of chicken, "and then you make excuses for her. 'But who knows what I'd be like if I were in a chair?" He mocks, quoting me. "Each to their own," he continues. "Everyone's different, I guess," he chuckles, then turns to meet my eyes.

He's right. I don't know what to say.

I frown.

"Don't worry. It's nice. I love that about you," he smiles, nudging my side with his shoulder. "I can just tell it's really hard sometimes."

13

Anna counts down again, as I hold the passenger door firm while she holds it and attempts to pull herself to a standing position from her wheelchair. Her legs don't move at all from her chair as she flops back into her seat.

"Urgh. They're not having it today!" she sighs in defeat.

"Maybe you'll just be doing the kids' Christmas shopping this year," she suggests, indicating that we're not going out to Kenmore Village shopping centre even though we've just spent the last forty-five minutes perfecting her updo hairstyle and filling in her eyebrows.

"Let's give it another go," I coax, repositioning myself out of the usual position to get further behind her. "I'm going to hold your feet from sliding out beneath you, and if you get your butt up enough, I'll push you upright from there, okay?" I strategise.

"No, if I can't get in the car now, then I'm going to be worse at the end of shopping. I won't be able to get in the car."

I recollect our bags from the boot, and turn off the car that I'd been cooling with the air conditioning. We head back inside. As we get back to the kitchen, I wonder what will now be ahead for our day, with Anna dressed and ready, but with her plans suddenly changed.

I stand at the head of the island bench, as we begin to discuss how we should fill our day ahead. As I'm standing there, I see my phone begin to ring.

"It's my dad," I announce to Anna. "Hmm, I should get that. Mum always calls, not Dad," I explain as I slide to answer. "Hey, Dad!" I answer, excited for his call.

"G'day, Special. How ya going?" he asks in a strangely genuine way, not like his usual general conversation.

"Yeah, I'm good. You?"

Where is this conversation leading?

"Yeah, I'm good. What are you up to?" he asks.

"Ah, not much actually. Anna and I were heading out today, but…" I look to Anna as I search for how to otherwise explain that she couldn't transfer into the car. "We've decided it was a bit much. So, we're chilling at home now, wondering what we'll do with our day," I explain politely to fill him in.

"Oh, there you go. Well, sadly, Special, I don't have good news."

He knows I'm at home and in just as good a position as ever to hear what follows. "Ash took his life last night."

A silence follows.

"*Our* Ashley?" I ask in shock.

"Yes, our Ashley. I'm sorry, Special," he follows quietly.

I feel my elbows press heavily into the bench as my entire body weight falls over the kitchen counter.

"What? No. Oh no," I blurt in disbelief, as my body moves to find ways to compute the shock.

"What? Why?" I question. I hear Dad catch his breath on the other end of the line.

"No one will ever know, Special," he says, attempting to comfort me.

My mind begins to move quickly between the shock and sadness of the immediate news, as I imagine my happy, positive, smiling cousin who has decided to leave us. The more I see flashes of his smiling face and memories shared together from childhood to now, the weight of my body becomes heavier, and the shock gives way to bursts of tears.

"I just spent a whole day with him in Kingscliff," I cry, even though I know Dad knows that.

"I know, Special, you're lucky you got to spend that time with him," he says, inadvertently expressing his own sadness of not having a recent moment with his nephew.

"Yeah, but we laughed all day. He was fine," I cry. "…He was happy," I continue.

"Well, you'll always have that memory of him, Special."

Dad tries to comfort his heartbroken daughter.

"I just don't get it," I say urgently. I straighten my posture. I feel my body change its state. I need more information from my dad. I ask him for more details on how Ash left this world, with my feet firmly planted beneath me. As I listen to Dad recount the facts of the previous night, I become acutely aware of my surroundings. I glance at Anna. She's got her head over her phone, and I notice that she's managed to open and finish her container of pears.

It catches me off guard, as she always asks for help with that tight seal.

I continue listening to Dad recount Ash's last moments. Preparing dinner for his partner, Shaji, in their home. *They opened their home to Jake and me on countless occasions.* The stark contrast between Ash's care for others to the tragic reality of his absence settles heavily. As I absorb my dad's words, I watch Anna quietly wheel herself behind me and open the fridge. In all my time here, I had rarely seen her retrieve anything from the fridge on her own. It lands with me strangely. Her quiet independence against my sudden helplessness.

I move myself toward a chair in the kitchen, situated opposite Anna. The conversation with my dad grows increasingly tiring and punctuated by moments of silence. He's now mostly listening as I sift through fragments of memories and conversations I've had with my kind and generous cousin.

Dad suggests I take it easy for the afternoon and reassures me I can call him whenever I need to. As I hang up, an overwhelming sense of loneliness settles in. I glance at Anna, awaiting her questions, and confidently assume that she's been able to gather what's happened from overhearing the conversation.

"I'm so sorry, honey, you're going to make me cry!" she says immediately, reaching for my arm across the table. Her words pull me sharply back into the present moment, engulfing me in a tangle of emotions. In my fragile state, it's as though my grief, raw and deeply personal, is no longer mine. My pain is not centred on me anymore. A part of me knows she's trying to connect, but all

I can feel in this moment is a loss of space for my pain. I need to be held, not to hold.

♥

It's Christmas Day, and I think of how it's such a perfect coincidence that the only Christmas I don't have anything special to eat, or a single thing planned, or am around anyone who truly cares for me, is the Christmas I'm physically unable to smile. There are so many oozing wounds inside my mouth that I'm unsure where one ends and the next one starts.

It's physically impossible to omit my smile without splitting one ulcer that starts at the root of my front bottom teeth, extends along the inside of my bottom lip and covers part of my bottom lip. I check my phone again to see if Noah has messaged me. I'm hopeful that at one point soon, he will realise that he's forgotten to invite me to his family Christmas. It's not his fault; he has a lot on his mind. Really, we're still in the early stages of getting to know each other. He wouldn't know how important this day is to me. I begin to think about the unnecessary pressure we put on ourselves at this time of the year. We feel obligated to complete every moderately large project we've ever started and to visit every single friend before Christmas, for no apparent reason, as if to say that catching up in January will be any different.

I feel like a drink, but I'm almost certain this headache I've had for two months now is because I'm drinking too much. Every morning, I wake with a tight band that grabs tightly from temple to temple. It softens ever so slightly by the time I'm needed to clock on with Anna. *I could pour a wine. Better yet, just grab the whole bottle.* But I'm nervous to leave my room. I'm torn. *Drinking water is painful enough, so will wine be any different? Maybe if I swirl the cheap bottle of red around my mouth for long enough, the alcohol will begin to soothe and numb the wounds?* I'm unsure if it's the logic of that theory, most certainly having only a slight effect, or the dread of opening my door that keeps me motionless and still on my bed. I do not want to open my bedroom door. I don't want Anna to hear me and give her any permission to ask for something else. I know exactly what she'd want at this time of day. It's late morning, and she's treating this day, Christmas Day, as if it's just another day. She'll want her nuts, and that's just another fiddly and exhausting job I haven't been able to get done. Getting her nuts isn't just a matter of passing her a packet of nuts. It's an ordeal involving me having to hand-pick all the almonds from a natural mixed bag and disperse them into a container, while also adding a perfect ratio of Brazil nuts and macadamia nuts. No more, no less, because I'll hear about it.

Macadamia nuts are so expensive, and they're even more expensive when you're required to find the cheapest packet in the suburb of Kenmore, meaning you'll spend two hours travelling to all three shopping centres. The expense that Anna cannot see is the cost of my sanity. It's a no-brainer for me. You pay the extra $3 at the supermarket you're shopping at, because the time it takes to drive to the other supermarket, find a park, walk inside and pay, those have then cost far more than $3. I often think that if Anna were the one physically doing these errands herself, she might weigh the cost differently. But it's been years since she's had to manage those kinds of tasks, and her focus is on the price on the shelf rather than the unseen toll it takes to chase it down.

I know what I'll do. I should get some fresh air for a while and call my family. My bedroom is at the front of the house, so I can swiftly open my bedroom door and hit the loud green open button for our automatic front door. So loud that it announces, 'I'm out of here!' rather than, 'I'm off to the kitchen, should you need anything.' It looks like a normal front door, but the button allows Anna to nudge it with her hand and immediately unlatch it loudly. It then swings inwards very slowly, allowing Anna enough time to relocate her wheelchair to be out of harm's way.

In one swift movement, I leave my room, grabbing Maddie's bird from my side table. She's restless from watching me lie motionless for hours. I hit the front door button whilst tossing her on the couch, and I slink stiffly out the front door. I stand at attention outside the house, kicking out my sore legs and hoping they'll soon regain sensation. I need to ensure the door is completely shut, with the bird inside the house. Because she, too, has been planning her escape from that house for as long as I've been there. We lock eyes for a second as if we both understand the need for freedom. I'm reminded that I can't even smirk at this stupid bird because my mouth is rancid.

I begin up the street, and for a second, I forget it's Christmas. I'm reminded when I can hear an unusual number of voices from one otherwise lonely house in the street, another has cars parked and strategically packed on the nature strip. A joyful young man, uncle in nature, is retrieving a washing basket, possibly full of presents and food, from the back seat of a car. His hands, now full with the basket, are somewhat restricting my view of his loud shorts. He spots me and gives me a smile that looks like he would only offer to a stranger in the street on one day of the year:

Christmas. The smile somehow also confirms to me that he'd only wear those shorts on one day of the year: Christmas. That gesture fills me with just enough spirit to reach for my phone and call my mum.

Mum quickly answers in what sounds like a scurry. I can hear her quickly slide open the door that divides our kitchen from the outside dining area.
It's probably right on lunch time. It's a bad time to call.

Even though I can hear Mum's hurried movement, her voice still sounds genuinely interested in my day and everything I've been up to. I try to make it sound more exciting than it was. I explained the trials I went through last night to build Maddie's new art and craft desk, complete with an easel attachment, in silence and for the first time ever played the important role of Santa. I explained how exhilarating it was to prop myself on the hard Velcro-like carpet and attempt to build a bike for the first time in my life. I'm warmed again by the thought of how exhausted and pained I was last night, yet being the only one responsible for keeping childhood magic and innocence alive was an honour that filled every cell in me, even the pus-filled ulcers.

I don't mention the ulcers to my mum; I just recount the magic of last night and how special those few minutes of this morning were. How magic it was that Anna had broken free of her prisoner routine and allowed me to get her out of bed early, keep her in pyjamas, wheel her out to the lounge room to watch her babies, Maddie and Ava, squirm with urgency to unwrap their gifts. How magically I anticipated the boiling kettle to stop, so I could pour Anna, Leah and me a coffee and enjoy it together. And how magic it was that all five of us were not only together, but together in excitement. When the story of that hour was over and my mouth began to make me wince, I quickly reverted to asking Mum what was cooking for lunch, as if it were going to be any different from the last twenty-four years of my life.

It wasn't.

"There's pork in the Weber, an assortment of salads, my tomato bake with breadcrumbs and all the trimmings," she listed quickly. I knew I couldn't talk to her for as long as I'd like to.

I thought she was moving around from room to room so quickly because she was tending to the food before I realised she was quickly trying to relocate the phone to the wider family.

"Hello to Karlee," she proclaims, and I can immediately hear my relaxed extended family. I can hear from the echoed voices that they're down in the shed. It's a nice day with the double doors wide open; everyone is far more relaxed than Mum. Billy's the closest voice to the phone, and I can hear he's got a minimum of two VB beers glow about him.

"Hello Karlee Warlee!" his voice is so close now that I know he's holding the phone.

'G'day Bill! What ya doin'?" I ask as though I've not got a skerrick of an idea.

"Ahh, just having a couple of beers, and Scarlett's telling us all how to play darts," he responds, which quickly prompts wider banter and a muffled, quick-witted smartass one-liner from Scarlett that suggests Billy isn't being a very good student at all. Caitlin asks me how I'm doing, so she has permission to ignore her child's comment.

"Yeah, I'm good," I lie. Dad's closer to the phone now.

"Hello Spesh!" He joyfully whips, and I check my forehead to make sure there's not actually a band stretching between my temples. Clenching my teeth as I wince in pain, the ulcer on my bottom lip rips open.

'Hello!" I deliver with an exceptionally deceitful sparkle.

"Good day?" He insists because he knows I'd never declare otherwise.

"Yeah, it's alright, but I'd love to be down there too!" I say, reaching for my lip. As if to assure him, I'm torn between two places, when the only thing that's torn is my lip. It's bleeding now. I'm distracted by the blood and unsure if I've missed a question or not.

"How's Uncle J?" I wonder, perhaps now thinking I'd heard his voice.

"Good Karlee girl! What's the weather like?" I'm refreshed by the question, but then quickly depressed by the facts.

"It's a perfect day up here!" I'm now listening to the world around me, and I can hear splashes in a pool and clinks of crockery as meals are transported outside in a nearby backyard.

"What's on for the rest of the day?" Now I'm really back in my own world. I need to end this phone call. I'm hurting now.

"Ah, not too much, well, listen, I just wanted to say hello to everyone, and wish everyone Merry Christmas! Mum's got lunch happening in a minute by the sounds of it, so I'll let you all go."

This convincing and reassuring tone is far too rehearsed and familiar. I'm disappointed now, though, because I thought I'd stopped doing that. I thought I'd stopped lying to them about the disaster that's happening around me. A harmony of goodbyes and well wishes is cast across the shed, and I hang up the call at the end of my street.

I continue through the shortcut and try not to think about the food they're about to enjoy. Regardless, I couldn't eat it anyway with this mouth. I'm momentarily proud of myself as I see the far signage of the local dentist. I get closer and hope for an A4 page to be stuck to the door showing their holiday hours. Relieved, they're open tomorrow. I'll do something about my mouth tomorrow, I promise myself.

I check my phone again and wonder what I'm meant to do now. It's so hot, it's too hot to venture down to the Gold Coast, and my car's air conditioning is officially not working. I'm somewhat worried about the pain across my head and whether I'd be safe to drive at this moment. I see a brief vision of coming off the M1 too quickly at the Carrara exit and crashing my car into the back of the green Mattress shop in Nerang, then a flash to my family being notified of my death on Christmas Day. I decide I won't go anywhere.

A glass of red wine really isn't going to cut it today. I need something colder and stronger, I think. I begin heading towards the bottle shop when I get to the traffic lights. They're unusually quiet. No cars in sight, not a single car. I begin to cross the road and almost twist my knee an entire 360 degrees when my heavy foot plants on the hot tarmac at the same moment I remember it's Christmas. I take a moment to clutch my shocked and twisted knee, and I'm reminded I'm in the middle of the road when I have a vision of being hit by an oncoming and quiet bus. Everything is quiet. Everything will be shut. I can't even buy anything cold and strong. Not even some Coles deli potato salad. I stand at the traffic lights, not another lonely soul as far as I can see, and there's actually nothing I can buy to help my head or heart at this minute. *If I had a cigarette, I'd smoke it. If anyone were here selling drugs, I'd buy them.* I start heading back to the house, and I wonder if, by some miracle that Kia has somehow managed to escape, and maybe my afternoon would then be filled with something worthwhile, hunting for a bird that I don't even like that much.

The door opens loudly, and I'm reminded of the reason why I left the house in the first place. It was because I couldn't bear to walk to the kitchen. I make a dash to the kitchen and hear Anna's bed creak ever so slightly. I can tell her hydraulic bed is almost entirely flat, and she's been asleep. I have the smallest window to get anything I need from the kitchen before retreating to the bedroom. I grab the bottle and the only nice wine glass in the cupboard, then quickly gather a plate with whatever food is easiest to grab. In a matter of seconds, I've armed myself with wine and something to eat, and I hurry back to my room. The bird chirps loudly as I pass, but I slip inside my bedroom quickly, food and wine balanced and grateful for the small win of retreat.

It's 2pm on Christmas Day, and I'm only just about to pour myself a drink, alone. I resubscribe to Netflix because I either need to take a pill that will wake me up in the morning or watch Gilmore Girls.

14

I'm at the dentist early, after going for a coffee first at the only place in town that serves it with heart and not by a moody 15-year-old. I immediately feel like crying when I reach the front desk of the reception. It's 9am. I've given them the first half hour of their day to answer the urgent people, but I figured I was up there, too. I struggle to express what I'm here for. I eventually get all the details out. Some of it is obvious, like the deep, bloody cut that runs through the middle of my bottom lip and the dry, peeling skin I attempted to clean and tidy earlier, but gave up on as I made more of a mess. To my surprise and relief, she explains that the dentist can possibly see me now if I'm happy to wait a moment.

It isn't even a moment, not one long enough to gather my thoughts before I'm walking into the dentist's chair. I realise I haven't been to the dentist since I was a child. *This is going to be horrible*. I also haven't been able to open my mouth wide for about eighteen months, since I dislocated my jaw yawning. The important files in my brain are being shuffled, and I can't tell which is the most important by the time the dentist speaks.

"How can I help?" she asks.

Tears. Nothing but tears and ache, and not much sound comes from me.

"I need help," is all that falls from my mouth.

I can't remember verbalising my fear of dentists or being picked and prodded, but somehow that's all soothed when the female dentist calmly puts her gloves on, pushes the trolley of daunting tools far away and holds up her bare, empty, gloved hands.

"Can I take a look?" She politely asks, hands tool-free in the air.

I lick my lips to lubricate them as they stretch over my teeth and allow my mouth to open. Ever so slightly, she touches the corner of my mouth and pulls it aside to shine her light in. She quickly comforts my stress before apologising.

"There's nothing I can do today."

I'm relieved.

"I think it's your wisdom teeth, at least the big ulcers at the back suggest so, but I'll need to confirm that with X-rays."

I begin crying again, because it's nice to hear someone speak so surely and accurately about my health.

I've been visiting my lovely GP for a few months now, and I was so deflated when the latest round of blood results came back all clear. I'm certain there was an underlying reason for the headaches or why I was passing blood on the toilet each morning. There's got to be a reason why the second round of antibiotics didn't clear up the infected wound on my foot. I wondered if the dentist was reading my mind.

"What's the name of your GP?" she asks.

I have to spell it out, and I feel horrible about it. I'm not confident in how to pronounce it, but I figure spelling it is better than rudely butchering it.

The dentist lights up upon hearing her name.

"They're open today, let's see if we can get you in," she announces brightly.

"I've got to be at work by ten," I say, only to realise it's only 9.04am and I have plenty of time. This whole visit has taken less than five minutes.

Next thing I know, I'm on my way around the corner to my lovely Indian GP. She is so kind and sweet, but I almost hold her accountable for my poor health, with no cause. The usually rude girl at reception greets me by name and with a smile as I walk slowly through the door.

What? She never does that.

I barely have time to answer her before I see my lovely Indian friend greeting me in the hall. She always seems angelic and peaceful. We do the usual greetings as we travel into position in her room.

As if she can hear me trying to organise the files in my brain again, she starts talking first this time. She starts speaking very slowly and seemingly informed. She says she's spoken to the dentist, and I can sense that she now feels sure about my health too.

Damn, that dentist was good.

My doctor summarises what needs to happen with my teeth

and the X-Ray, and begins to explain what I can get and do for my mouth wounds. For the first time, I begin to cry to her. Her certainty feels comforting. Her matter-of-factness feels like the big hug I've always wanted from her. I feel free to fall apart now in the absence of her normal pleasantries and manners. She surely and precisely looks at her screen and hits print. I am expecting a script for another antibiotic. She carefully grabs the paper from her tray and gently touches the pages as if she is feeling for the words to explain what she is about to say next.

"I'd like you to take a moment to answer all these questions. Don't think too long, just answer them."

I begin the quiz and answer every question independently. The questions are about different aspects of my life, and I haven't really stopped to think about any of them. *How was my sleep? How was my appetite? Am I energised? Am I finding it difficult to stay focused?*

All seem quite general in nature until I read the next few. The band on my temples pulled tighter, and I feel a loose piece of my lip flap shakingly as I exhale heavily.

Do I think about dying? I start feeling uncomfortable. I can't answer them.

I'm just going through a hard time; I'm not sick. Ash was sick, I'm not. I can't be. I can't hurt our family more. I'm just not happy; I'm not mentally ill. I'm working really hard. I've been through far worse times. Looking after Jake was hard and lonely, but this is fine. I have a great boyfriend. I'm just tired. Anna's negativity is just wearing me down. I'm just staying until March, then I'll have lived up to my promise of caring for Anna for a year. I'm just a bit tired. I've just got this stupid head pain and, ulcers and something wrong with my gut. I'm not depressed.

"Just answer them truthfully for me, Karlee. Don't overthink it," she says kindly.

I catch my breath and just do as my stern, certain and kind doctor tells me to. The questions that follow all seem to be of the same kind. With every question about life or death, I visualise my doctor opening a door inside my brain. It's like a limestone cave, except it's the dripping gems that are the tissue of my brain. She swings a door open in the cave, shines her torch in to look for anything, then closes the door. She continues down the cave's corridor, another question, another door. She walks more urgently to each door, and they all lead to dark corners, with nothing. The test is finished.

She begins looking at the responses. I watch as her body shifts in consistency, one second hard, then the next second soft. Hard to soft, hard to soft. She holds the white square pages, gently flicking the corners. I follow the page edge as she moves the test from suspended in the air to flat on her desk. The top left corner grabs my attention. I stop biting the dry, loose flesh of my lip and begin to trace the page, top left across to the right corner, down along to the bottom right corner, across and back up again. I begin to lap the page edge again with my sight before my kind doctor interrupts my tracing.

"Karlee, you've returned results that express highly anxious tendencies and depression." She pauses to await my reaction, but it's just silence as we both sense relief for the elephant in the room.

"You sure I don't just have cancer?" I smirk as more relieving tears begin to line my face. Her body begins to soften with my reaction and then hardens just as quickly from her toes to her head. Her face is the last part that hardens before she asks, "Do you know what is happening? What's troubling you?"

It doesn't take me a moment to begin my unravelling.

"I'm just so tired. I'm exhausted. I can't get rid of this headache. I know all the things to do to make me feel better, but they're just not working. And they're becoming impossible to do. No matter what time I wake in the morning, I feel like I need more sleep. And then I just can't handle working for Anna anymore. I used to be able to turn everything around and make it positive, but it's just ruining me. I can't catch a break from anything, the foot and now this mouth. As if my head couldn't hurt more, my mouth decides to gift me this shit for Christmas. I'm just so over it. I don't know what to do."

My doctor searches for the right words. I can tell she's organising her thoughts. I search the wall she's staring at. Her deep sigh tells me she can't help me in the way she'd like. I can physically see my words begin to hurt her; she softens again. I begin to think about my many recent visits and how I'd never troubled her before. I'd never kept her for this long before either. I always know what I need, so I just sit down there and lay out the facts. Usually, I just sit down and tell her what's physically wrong. The cuts are not healing, my gut is turning, and the antibiotics are making me ill in the morning. I begin to wonder if it is, in fact, all in my head. *Have I caused all of this myself?* I check the wall again and get interrupted by my doctor's stare.

"You need to make some drastic changes, Karlee. You need to leave this job," she says. I feel that truth in the bottom of my gut. *She's right.* She makes it sound so simple. *It's really not that simple.*

"I promised Anna I would be there for a year," I plead.

"You're damaging yourself; you're not helping anyone by being this unwell. We'll get you all the help you need. Something for your ulcers today, your X-ray next week, and a splint for your jaw. Wisdom teeth out, but before all of that, you need to speak with a mental health professional. They can help you with strategies to cope, to unwind a little in times of high tension. We have some great help here in Kenmore or in Toowong."

She begins tapping at her computer. "If you're happy to travel to Toowong, we can book you in for your days off, sound okay?"

"Okay. I can do that." My ulcer cracks open as I smile. *She remembers my days off.*

As she begins to tap away at her keyboard, I reach for my phone to check the time. It's nearly 10am, so I message Anna to let her know I've been held up at the chemist. "Oh, magnesium!" I remember Anna needed more magnesium. I'm slightly comforted that I can be late yet still spend her time getting her something. I wipe my leftover tears from my cheek and stow away my phone. The doctor gathers her envelopes and signs the foot of each letter. She nudges one toward me as she reaches for the script and begins to sign that.

I read the first and last line:

'Thank you for seeing Miss Hayes for treatment of Depression and anxiety...'

'Please assist in sharing your findings in order to support Karlee moving forward.'

My doctor kindly takes the letter, folds it neatly, and slips it inside the envelope. I'm distracted when I see her arm reach for me from the corner of my eye. I stare at her soft, milky palms, surprised she's not passing me something, until I see her hand find my forearm. She gently takes hold of my arm.

"You'll get through all of this, and there's so much help. You can come in here whenever you need to, okay?" she assures me. She's so lovely.

I walk out again straight past the front counter, giving my usual, 'That's all good?' Again, I'm shocked by the reception girl who offers an out-of-the-ordinary, 'Take care, Karlee, see you next time.' I leave slightly frustrated as to how this woman finds kindness for someone only after knowing they're having a mental breakdown. I'm sure now that the dentist must have made the call and expressed the urgency of my appointment.

I wander next door to the chemist and immediately head for the prescriptions counter. While waiting for my script, I browse the pharmacy shelves, slowly closing in on the magnesium. I examine every item and assess how it might benefit Anna. I consciously scan the cupboard at home for any containers that are getting low. I think for the most part, we're stocked. I spot some Paw Paw ointment and immediately feel the thirst of my bottom lip. Grabbing my lip, I remember what I need to do. *I need to be quick… How am I going to find the courage to quit?*

♥

The cheese is sweating on the board. So am I. I stare at the carrots I nervously cut to perfection, hoping they might start a conversation that shifts us away from home improvements. Anna sips her wine. I want to, too. She's only drinking on this occasion, our belated Christmas drink. I save my sip to soften another pause.

"That Dracaena should be centred over there." She starts on about the garden. "Can't you see that?"

I grab a carrot, chew it slowly, as I turn my body toward the potted plants.

"Oh yeah! I can see that from here." I try to keep my tone light. "I'll spend some time out here tomorrow, because I think they all need moving slightly left. They're not getting any morning sun."

It's meant to be my day off, but I know by now that rest and Anna's ideas often overlap.

"Or we could repot those few that are getting too big," she continues, her train of thought unbroken.

A quiet part of me pleads she doesn't mean right now. My energy, already stretched thin from the least festive December I've ever had, feels as though it's evaporating out here in the afternoon heat and her endless plans.

♥

I stand at Anna's bedside in the late afternoon hours. Her blinds are drawn to restrict the strong afternoon sun from beaming into her room.

"How'd you go?" Anna asks.

"Yeah, okay, I guess…" My voice trails off, searching for the words that need to be said.

"I need to get my wisdom teeth removed," I explain with upset and fear beginning to bubble in my throat.

"Oh, honey, that's okay," she says gently, as though she can handle that amount of absence.

"It needs to be done soon, as they believe my jaw tension is possibly all due to the pressure." My words tumble out quickly. "I just think I need to do it soon, and probably take that chance to finish up, so I can have some time to recover."

"Finish up?" Anna questions softly.

"Yeah. Finish up working here. I'm sorry. I'm just not well," I confess, now crying with overwhelm.

"Oh, honey, I know. You haven't been yourself for some time now."

As I fight back more tears, her comment lingers, cutting deep even though I know she means it with concern.

Does she mean I haven't done a good enough job caring for her? Or the kids? Does she have any idea that that's ALL I've been doing this whole time?! Pouring every ounce of myself into them and leaving nothing for myself? Does she realise how much I've struggled here doing this role for several months now? The only reason I've stayed this long is to spare her kids the pain of yet another unreliable live-in nanny, the kind who barely lasts three months, compared to my eleven. *I can't do this anymore. I need to leave.*

15

I don't think it's the pain from my wisdom teeth extraction that is keeping me lying in my late teenage bedroom. I can't fathom getting out of bed to see my parents. The kindest, most supportive and caring people I know. I know that this is exactly where I need to be right now, as I let the swelling subside from my surgery. But the weight I'm carrying inside seems far heavier than just these swollen cheeks.

My parents would be nothing but understanding. They'd let me cry, they'd let me wallow in this space for a while. Then, they'd help me find clarity, reminding me that my problems might not be as big as they seem. But I don't want to worry them. *How much would it hurt to know your kind and intelligent daughter just doesn't feel like either of those things? That she doesn't want to leave her bedroom, much less take a step forward.*

THE ART OF ~~LIVING~~ GIVING | 163

I don't even know if I want to go back to Brisbane, or anywhere else for that matter. Everything feels too much, today, tomorrow and all the days after. Right now, all I want is to close my eyes and drift away.

♥

"You look different from your picture," says Aiden, the man who advertised for a carer, with more detail about the physical attributes of his ideal new employee than the job itself. He stares at me.

"Okay…" I swallow mixed emotions. He can hardly think any worse of me than I think of myself right now. But I did try to present well in this interview. I really need some money. *Don't worry about it. Just get the job and earn enough to pay rent.*

"I think you had your hair down in the picture," he insists, referring to the photo that was demanded in the ad. 'Don't apply unless you attach a photo,' it said.

So he really is as heartless as the ad sounded.

"You're not normally the type of person I would hire," he says sheepishly, as though he's chosen his words carefully.

What? Ugly?

"But you have a lot of experience across lots of fields. Marketing, HR, management." He can't make eye contact with me.

So I'm unattractive but smart? Am I here to care for you or run your business?

"Do you eat meat?" He asks.

What the bloody hell does that have to do with things?

"Yes, I do."

"Oh, good. I need someone to cook me a steak. The girl who works the evening shift at the moment is a bloody vegan. Cat. She's absolutely gorgeous. Sadly, a lesbian. But she won't cook steak for me." He looks to me as if he's just talked about steak, and not another woman's personal affairs.

"Right, okay. I can cook steak." I hold back my discomfort.

"Well, can you come for a trial shift tomorrow night?"

Now's my chance to run and not hear anymore insults about myself or others. But I need a job. It pays well. I can handle some insults.

"Sure. Anything you need me to know or do before then?" I enquire.

"Just meet me at my apartment, I'll send the address. Don't look so professional. Wear something nice…" He looks around the room searching for his next words.

"Look more like your resume photo."

Arsehole.

"Got it," I say with a smile. "See you tomorrow."

I grab my handbag and head out of his office room door. As I walk away from the man, I feel my lungs filling with air, growing deeper. Calmer. My mind conflicts.

I don't have to go tomorrow. I'm employable and can get another job. But I could just do this job. It pays really well. Just two four-hour shifts are enough to pay the rent of my newly found unit in Mermaid Beach, on the Gold Coast. It'll give me a break. Enough time to prepare for more insults from him. I'll do it.

By the time I reach my car parked out on the street, I've convinced myself the job isn't good for me. A disaster waiting to happen. But again, I spiral.

Why shouldn't I help him? He's probably never had someone call him out on his behaviour. He's probably never had any genuine carers in his life before. Anyone with half a brain would run from this. I should help him.

♥

It's a Friday, and most people my age in my position are torn for things to do. I should feel torn, too. I should feel more than I do right now, anything in fact. I should feel something.

The view from our balcony offers a glimpse into many different worlds. You can see the smallest glimpse of the ocean meeting the sky, but only when visibility allows it. Having only the smallest window of ocean view gives a new perspective to the deep blue sea. The small laser-focused frame gives me something to compare its colours to.

On one side, the view is framed by a high white concrete high-rise, something that would have been different in the 1970s. The other is a showcase dream home for a family. With kids who I imagine have no idea what hard work looks like. Kids who would never associate with anyone raised differently.

From this raised first-floor vantage point, I can see over their high walls and almost trace the floor plan. It's confusing. In the vision I've created, there are courtyards and glass walkways connecting one part of the home to the other. A second-floor room is covered entirely with wood panelling. Hard damaged by the ocean. Frequently varnished. No windows. I used to think the room was a theatre, but now I know it's a sheltered room to hang their laundry.

No sun damage for the designer clothes. No neighbours see their dirty laundry. Just a steady breath of air slipping through the timber slats. The image of air moving through the gaps tightens my own chest.

Stop it. You're out here to catch your breath.

I have my phone nearby, a catalogue of people I know, many who I know do love me, but many I can't call. What would I say?

Hi, I don't know what's wrong with me. Hi, I can't stop thinking about aliens because I now believe it's possible for something so physical and conscious to exist yet to have no feeling at all. Hi, how are things with you? Don't tell me about the person annoying you at work. I don't care. Hi, you're going to have to do all the talking because I don't have anything to say. Hi, I know I should've called. I am now. Hi, yeah, I've tried going for a walk.

I truly understand why people don't talk; why our heads are the silent killers: it's because they are silent. When things are working fine, the brain's like a tapestry, woven with emotion and thought. Moving in response and connection to the world around you. But mine has been blank for months. I know what to say and how to function, that's all in my muscles, but there is nothing new.

Hope, I've concluded, is newness. Hope is forward-thinking, having plans, and wanting to see what happens. This state is free of hope. It's hopeless.

I used to start my mornings visualising. Seeing and hoping for the future. I sat in silence that breathed clarity into my day. But lately, all I see is the cave. The limestone cave. Not glowing, not warm. Just echoing, empty, and cold. The cave was once full of corridors and dripping crystal walls. Behind each wall, I believed I might find Karlee. Tied up in a straitjacket, just wanting to be freed.

She's in here somewhere. I just have to keep looking.

My new flatmate, Hannah, would help me find the door of humour. Brilliant! I'd open it wide. Hoping that Karlee, one who loved to laugh, was in their hiding. Although I hadn't found her there, I'd feel a waft of her energy in the air. A trace. Enough to make a joke, to smile at something stupid. But those wafts don't last long. Each time I open a door, the draft of amusement, empathy, joy, fear, sadness, curiosity, all escape. Eventually, the doors disappear. The walls do too. Just one open cavity. A room of just empty chairs. A circle of empty chairs, like some kind of therapy session. The rest are vacant unless a different version of me works up the courage to join.

Running helps. One element of the old morning routine I can do. When I run, that seated version of me relaxes. She softens. She stops scanning the room. After each run, I'd sometimes find a new version of me. She'd be unlacing her shoes, proud. Amazed at how far we ran. She speaks in a way that says, 'We'll do it again tomorrow.'

Tomorrow. That's hope. We sit together. She wriggles her toes. She lingers long enough to inspire something. A meal, perhaps. Or a visit to my surfer boyfriend. The walk to Noah's place isn't far. That's why I moved here. I take the runner version of me along. And excitement too.

Noah's not often doing anything. He's fresh from a surf or watching YouTube in bed. I join in. I tell him about my run. About how sore my silly hips are. He tells me soreness isn't good. He tells me I shouldn't run. That running isn't good for me. The runner in me quietly gets up and leaves. Excitement does too.

Now it's just me, in the circle, alone. Noah's silence makes it easier to stay quiet. I never picture him in a chair, but I feel him. Lying on his chest, I imagine his brain was never an intricate cave. He has always been in a single room, full of chairs. All full. All versions of him are always yelling, always at war with himself. It's why he's always resting. It's why he's quiet. It's why he never wants to do anything. It suits me. I don't know what I want to do either.

We eat. That's one thing. He's always hungry. It makes me eat too. Sometimes we buy wine. We always drink it all. And if ever we buy too much, I notice it's gone the next time I visit. He drinks the rest alone. The nicest thing he does is bring me coffee in bed before he leaves for work. White, with honey and a kiss. That's when gratitude quietly takes her seat. The sun pours through his windows. Bird song. The hush of Mermaid Beach. Then he says he loves me. Love takes a seat. I feel ready for the day. He leaves, and I roll over and lie in his sunlit bed. I'm warm. Breathing easy.

Eventually, I head home to my unit. I tell myself I'll apply for a new job. *Something easier. Something where I'm not insulted for how I look or how I cut his steak.*

I open my clunky old laptop. I bought it back in high school. With each lag, gratitude grunts. Love fidgets. They get impatient and go. Now, the room is empty again. A half-written cover letter stares back at me.

How do I write about myself when no one is home? I'm not a hotel manager; I'm not a HR specialist. I'm just here. I wouldn't hire me, so why would anyone else?

Even the thought of any other job is exhausting. Get up, get dressed, be on time. Just thinking about it makes me tense. Most days, I go to work like this. Empty.

I used to think helping people would keep me connected to the world. But I'm losing touch instead. I shut the laptop. Stand up. Before I know it, I'm reaching for my bathers.

♥

I venture out of the house again, just before midday. It's the peak of the day, but it's nearing winter, so the sun doesn't feel like it ruins me. I walk on the hard sand near the water line.

I get started from my Wave Street entrance and head south, towards the Miami hill. I take a moment and genuinely ask myself what I need. *How far am I going?* I think of the cover letter again. I think about how I can't sell myself at this point in time. I see the dry limestone cave momentarily, but I refuse to take a seat there today. It's a good day.

I've had coffee in bed. I've been in the ocean. I've had a slow tea in the sunshine at home, and I'm now here on the beach with nowhere to be. I feel the urge to take action. *I can put on a podcast and have a laugh.*

I unlock my phone, and Instagram is still open. It shows me an old friend from high school and his cartoon face advertising his podcast. Sam Peterson was always funny and made everyone happy wherever he was. I think about how lucky I was to have witnessed a future comedian in his high school years.

I remember the last time I saw him. He was heartbroken, going through a breakup, yet he still made me laugh and feel good as his world crumbled around him.

I follow the links to his podcast and hit play. Coincidentally, the episode I'm listening to is paying reference to being on a beach. I settle into my surroundings. Sand, breeze, sun and distraction. What comes next catches me by surprise. Laughter. Genuine, heartfelt, roaring and uncontrollable. The laughter continues to grab onto each part of me. I land each step unsteadily on the sand. And for what feels like the first time ever, I look up. I look around to see other people. They're catching glimpses of me and smirking. *I must be contagious.* The strangers drop their heads with a smile after a moment of eye contact. It's as though my heavy and empty head had been impairing my peripheral vision. Unable to see the details of my surroundings. I'd only been looking directly ahead for months.

I continue walking with a smile. The smile feels as though it strains across my face. Reversing muscles that have been so strongly set in the opposite direction. I can still feel the tight band across my forehead, ready to snap. I continue to consciously hold my pleasant face and giggle intermittently at Sam's voice. I'm amazed. Even while Sam had been experiencing such heartache when I saw him last, he still carried himself so lightly.

I think about my previous months and realise I've done the

same. While I haven't consciously reached out to friends or kept in contact with them, those I have encountered have still received a fun and light-hearted version of me. *I don't know how to act otherwise.* I imagine the same rule applied to Sam. Kindness and positivity have become part of my identity. So much so that even when it hasn't reflected my insides, it has remained my only mode of operation. Everything on the outside has continued to function as it always has, despite the cold, empty, and dark cave I'm living in.

Feeling better for giving myself reason to laugh and now being carried with such lightness along the beach, I wonder if there's anything else I can give myself at this moment. Acknowledging that I haven't spoken to friends or reached out in some time, I decide that's what I should do. *I need to stop avoiding my friends.* Now, beyond the Miami hill and nearing Burleigh, I randomly scroll my phone's contact list. I see the name of an old primary school friend, Larissa. She has known me through many chapters. She expressed on social media recently that she has had some troubled times and that the worsening pandemic was making things harder. *She'd be a good person to speak to.*

I call her, holding my breath. After just a few rings, she answers. She sounds somewhat surprised to hear from me. I admit I'm just calling for no other reason than an overdue check-in. The conversation moves naturally, and I try to keep it off me. I quickly mention that I've left my role with Anna and the kids, and that I'm spending a bit of time cruising with minimal work. Seemingly uninterested, she shifts the conversation back to her world, which still features many of our high school friends. I'm pleased not to talk about my life. She speaks of our friends. Unaware that I've spent several years being unable to relate to them all. Dissimilar. Distant.

It's only moments of listening before I realise how much I had to grow up in the years I cared for Jake. *I'm unexcited by empty, young, nothing conversations. Disheartened by the bonds they all share. I don't feel like anyone I know.*

The relationships formed at school are based on exposure to the same thing. It's perfect proof that you are, in fact, the people you surround yourself with. *I was similar to them. Until I wasn't. I was the same as them. Able to connect with them. Right up until I left, left the small community and moved interstate for university. I was like them, until I was no longer experiencing anything like them. Now, it's equally true that they are unlike me, and I am unlike them.*

I begin to feel selfishly relieved to hear of Larissa's struggles in isolation. I wonder if she and our other high school friends might be more relatable now. *Will they relate to my loneliness? I can't decide what's more isolating: government restrictions imposed against your own will or upholding promises that you feel bound to by your own moral compass.* I conclude that time isolating in health, in a home you've made in health, supported by the government, is not at all the same as having your life crumble underneath you due to ill health. And made worse when you're not the sick one.

I continue to listen to Larissa address many of the friends I've drifted apart from, before her language begins to get sharp, narky, as though she's drifted from them too. The conversation begins to get so negative that, before long, I see the empty chairs inside. Her words begin to hurt. Her next line strikes me deep: "No one called me on my birthday."

I selfishly think back to my own birthday. I struggle to

remember anything that happened on my birthday. *Did anyone call me? Did I get any gifts? I don't even think there was cake.* I'm not upset about that. A bike, I got a second-hand rusty bike from Noah. I should have known. At least he got me something right? I really need to oil those brakes. I might ride it more if I weren't so ashamed of the squeak that woke every sleepy head in Mermaid Beach on Sunday morning.

"Like, how hard is it to leave a voicemail?" Larissa interrupts my thoughts.

Did she leave me a voicemail? Did I leave her a voicemail? I'm sure I did. Her birthday is April 17th; I'll never forget it. I fight every part of me that wants to defend myself. *I could've sworn I left a voicemail. No, I posted on her Facebook wall.*

"You know what, it doesn't even matter. There's no point holding onto things that don't serve you anymore." Larissa completes.

Unsure if I've said anything at all, I stop my quick steps on the sand. All I can see is the empty room inside my head. Just empty chairs. *Are there more chairs than before?* The tight band across my head feels tighter. My head begins to throb at a familiar pace. I feel the muscles in my cheeks tighten to their familiar distressed position. I instantly try and count the minutes I haven't felt like this. *How long have I gone without feeling my head?* It could have been hours. I reach for my phone to check the time. *It's only 1:15.*

The phone call ends with a whole heap of pleasantries that pour out from somewhere in me that remembers how to function. I've said what was needed to soothe and comfort Larissa. My feet slow to a halt. *I don't know what to do.* I lift my head toward the horizon and feel the muscles in my neck and shoulders stretch to warn me they've watched my feet for too long. My eyes are set on where the water meets the sky. *I want to be back on my balcony, where I have a little window with an ocean view. My balcony seems so far away right now. My hips are hurting. My head is hurting. I am hurting.*

My feet don't feel strong enough to carry my weight. I'd sit if my hips would let me fold to the ground. As one breath creeps inside my dry mouth, it feels caught on something sharp in my chest. I try that breath again, and the same thing repeats. Another dry breath tries to make its way deeper, but it can't get past the others. I realise now. *It's imperative that just one breath, at least one, finds my lower chest.* I attempt again, but despite this breath having my entire body's attention, it barely makes it past my throat.

There's a sharpness in my chest that tightens, despite any breaths making it that far. I'm frightened. *I really need a breath.* I clench my jaw, and I'm reminded of the big holes in my mouth. The sharp sensation grows across my chest, and my hands reach to feel for anything physically restricting. *It's like a thorny vine creeping and acquiring any vacant land on my body.* Looking back up to the horizon, I feel the stretch again. Those thorns are now ripping and tearing my back just to lift my head. The breath, now at the base of my throat, begins to feel like murky dishwater, rather than oxygen-filled air. It carries the same slime-like sensation that shocks and disrupts your skin at the end of the cleaning. *I want to be sick.* Every part of my body rejects the idea of allowing air any deeper into my body.

Now just a body. Standing shakily on a beach. Fragmented

into three different parts. A chest with limbs of piercing thorns, a throat carrying slimy dishwater air, and a mouth that is so parched that air ricochets off its walls and struggles to find a passage. My lips tear as they peel across my face to ask for air.

I now see myself from a vantage point thirty metres away. I'm hunched, one hand grabbed at my chest, lips stretched across my face, one hand on my slightly bent knees. I watch the entrance of a character. Swiftly, an aged beachgoer with embraced greys in her once sun-kissed hair approaches me. She bends down under my dropped head. Her gentle hands touch with the notion of having cradled the backs of her own children with care.

I meet her eyes. They look like mine. Her wrinkles around her eyes crinkle and change, suggesting she's speaking with urgency. I can't hear anything. I witness her eyes gloss over and feel my own do the same. The sensation of her hand on my back acts like a warm poison on the thorns that begin to let go of the muscles near her touch. I begin to hear her voice. She speaks as though she's known me forever.

"Honey, can you tell me what's happening?" My careful beach angel strains. "Please sit down, darling. Come on, let's sit down just here."

My eyes continue to gloss over, and my vision of her wrinkles becomes blurry. I feel her hand again as it warms the tense vine on my back. I know she has time to sit with me.

"Talk to me, darling, what's going on? I can help you." Her words are soft and gentle. I remember where I am.

"I can't breathe," I swallow a lump of dishwater.

"Oh, honey, it's alright, let's sit down." I can feel her trying to urge me to the sand. Her hand warms my back again, and I gasp for another breath.

16

It's been a month since Noah dumped me at the nearby dinner table. I lie on the floor, my legs heavy from having run plenty of kilometres to and from Broadbeach. My hips ache. 'Don't run anymore,' they beg. But my mind urges them on. It's worth it.

My bare feet are blistered. The only running shoe I own is a pair of heavy, battered Asics Netburner, from my under-15 netball days at Nyora. Footwear science has advanced significantly in the past decade. *Maybe I'll treat myself to some new runners, once I'm certain that I am a runner.* I open my scrapbook to a blank page and ask, 'How do I really want to spend my days?'

I search through my cave-like mind for any memories or things that recently lit me up. First to mind, a letter from Maeve. Pencil scribbled, joy-filled, addressed to me like I'm a celebrity pen pal. Not something you'd expect from a 23-year-old woman. She told me about her latest adventures, even down to her most recent cup of tea. *I love letters*, I conclude. *They bring me joy.*

Then I think of Hannah, my flatmate. My saviour through the breakup week. When shock turned to grief, grief turned to worry, then worry to red wine on the couch. Hannah walked in with armfuls of corn chips and a handmade coupon booklet.

Each coupon, a little permission slip. Wallow in bed for a day, dirty dishes left guilt-free, breakfast on her, judgement-free wine before midday. It wasn't just the thoughtful coupons. It was the words carefully written. Then, folded with care. *I love letters.*

Next, I think of flowers. The bunches that found me through hard seasons. Some from Anna and the kids when my cousin passed, from Martina at Christmas time, and from Alice when we finally reunited. Each ignited a little moment of joy. Enough to know that someone was thinking of me. But while I saw Earth's smile in the petals of each stem, I also saw their impending doom. *Wouldn't it be nice if flowers lasted a little longer?*

Flowers and letters, I thought, two things that light me up. *Am I meant to be a florist?* I picture myself penning heartfelt notes, tucking them into blooms, sending love from one human to another. But they die. *If only there were a bunch of flowers that lasted longer or better, one that grows.*

The thought sends me spiralling, in a good way. I search Pinterest for sustainable flowers and packaging. Craft paper. Earthy greens. Beautiful, bright, but a little muted. Like life. I think about dried flowers, how they are preserves of what's already lived. *But rather than give something that's holding on, let's give something that's growing. What if the gift is a bunch of flowers that grow?*

On the scrapbook page, I scribble, "You grow, girl!" I don't know where that phrase has come from, but it sticks. It sounds right.

I dive deeper. Sustainable packaging, cards and kits. Brands that carry emotions, not just aesthetics. I imagine a gift that doesn't die in four days. A gift that grows. A gift that reminds the receiver over and over that they are loved. And suddenly, there's colour again, not just on the page, but in the corners of my mind. There's hope.

♥

I race eagerly up the stairs of my Mermaid Beach unit, almost completely free of the tension from being around Aiden. I've been part of his care team for three months now, and while I didn't think I'd last this long on his team, I'm beginning to enjoy the role. I've exceeded my own expectations. All I need to do is turn up, cook him dinner and keep him company. It's the most guilt-free money ever. I just have to pretend to see eye to eye with him; that's the hard part. But the job keeps a roof over my head. Just eight hours a week, two short evening shifts a week, means I get to spend the rest of my days watching the sunrise over Mermaid Beach, running to Burleigh, having a coffee at the same table every morning at BSKT, the local cafe, then brainstorming my business idea for the rest of the day.

I'm eager to get home today, as I've just received my branding kit from the design team I hired to help bring my vision to life. We've been back and forth for weeks, now getting nearer and nearer to being on the same and completely new page. It's been the most thrilling experience, tweaking and experimenting to create and actualise something that was only in my head, with so much feeling. It's incredible that out of nothing, you can create something. Seeing the absence of something in their design has uncovered what I actually wanted there to start with.

We'd conceptualised brand names, toyed with the words 'You Grow Girl,' and worked on versions of that for a name, but I wasn't convinced it relayed the message entirely. The process made me look at brands and businesses like never before. It opened my eyes to what I liked, what drew me into other businesses. 'Why did I trust that brand?' I wondered as I watched TV or made a purchase. Within one list of brand names that the Melbourne-based design team delivered to me, one name stood out. It grabbed me the moment my eyes jumped across the words. I reread the three words again before reading them aloud. I stared at the name and loved how it looked, unaware still of what I saw in the brand or logo. I loved that these words sat above the line and had alliteration: Seed A Smile. That was it. I was certain of it.

Today, as I eagerly open the branding document, I'm preparing to see the rest of Seed A Smile's branding come to life. I'd decided on a logo, but next came the colours, and the rest of the vision. As I flick from page to page, I'm amazed by the colours and the typography that have completely adopted everything I had felt that day lying on the loungeroom floor, when this idea was born, as well as every ounce of research I'd made since. *Here it is, right in front of me.* A brand of bright pastels, that's punny and inspiring.

All right here, in front of my eyes. Something I've created, in the darkness of my own mind, in the hope that this brand will bring a little more light to the world. I can see now that it actually will.

I can envision the brand reaching people's doorsteps. I see friends reading the message on the card as they pull open every intricate detail of the package. I can see the green pastel tissue paper against the kraft box. I see the reusable finishes like the small calico-branded bag holding dehydrated soil, which is carefully untied and inspected. And most of all, I see the joy that the gift will bring to all those who receive it. It's perfect, I conclude, scrolling back through the pages to see my happy brand once again.

As the joy from this brand starts washing over me and encompassing my entire mood, I think to myself, 'here's a moment that's lit me up!' I reflect on how, just a month ago, I struggled to find even the smallest ounce of joy — and how *this* moment has been born from that. I've created this joy entirely on my own, outside the usual paths to happiness. I want to spend my days in ways that feel truly aligned. And the best thing about it all is that it's all for others. This gift will bring so much to others, yet look just what it's done for me.

♥

I stand at the wall of runners in Rebel Sports. Only one and a half hours into the drive home from the Glasshouse Mountains, where my brother Billy and I just spent four nights together at Spicers Retreat. Originally, I had planned to take Noah along for the romantic getaway, which thankfully doubled as a work trip.

My client Harry, whom I'd now been caring for in addition to Aiden for five months, had asked if I'd be happy to accompany him and his wife to the retreat, so they could have a nice break. I was absolutely delighted to do so. Planned long in advance, the trip became a little less sweet after Noah and I broke up. Harry was the one to suggest my brother Billy join me instead, and thankfully, Billy was able to arrange his days off from his new job near the mines in Mackay to drive down and meet me for the luxurious stay. We enjoyed our time together, relaxing in the wooden spa on our balcony that overlooked a little valley, playing guitar, and in the evening drinking many beers.

Billy and I spoke about our cousin Ash, acknowledging it had been almost a year since he'd left our world and crushed our hearts.

"I'd really like to do something in honour of him," Billy had proposed, breaking a long silence and interrupting both our recollections of happy memories.

So, as I stand wondering if I'm worthy or not yet to get a new pair of running shoes, I ring Billy. He answers quickly and with a dash of concern in his voice, knowing I've not long started my journey home to the Gold Coast.

"Karlee Warlee?" He answers.

"Hey Bull! Don't worry, I'm all good," I reassure him. "I've just stopped at Rebel Sports on my way home, and I'm standing here about to buy some runners. I really want to break them in quickly, to justify spending $183 on them!"

"Just buy them! Do you need me to lend you some money?" He quickly wonders and kindly offers.

"No, no. I'll buy them. I just want to make sure I don't get over this running phase, like, tomorrow. So, I was thinking, to honour

Ash, how about for the next month you contribute $1 for every kilometre I run to a charity that supports those with a mental illness?" I propose.

"Oh!" Billy sounds pleasantly shocked.

"It can be any charity or organisation, whatever you prefer. I'll do all the running and track it. I'll run a lot. And the more I run, the more you have to donate," I suggest competitively.

"Make it $2 every K you do then!" He competes.

"Right-o then!" I declare. "You're on! Do we have a deal?"

"Yep! Maybe Mum and Dad will do the same?" Bill suggests.

"Oh, true! Good idea. Right-o then. I'm going to buy these and get joggin' then!" I declare in motivation.

"Yep, go for it! Start charging me then, hey?!" Billy says cheekily.

"Yep, I'm going to drain your bank, Bill!"

"Well, I hope you do! Good on ya, Karlee Warlee. Speak soon!"

♥

I return to the seats on my balcony and unlace my shoes again. The rolls of blister tape sit on the table next to me, as I peel my no-longer-new Asics runners carefully off my feet. It felt like only minutes before that I'd put these shoes on, determined to go for another run to clock up more kilometres and raise more funds. This run was over before it even began. Unlike my hips or knees, I've just learnt that blisters aren't a pain that gets better the more you warm them up. It's not like the aches I've experienced now for nine days straight. The ache I wake with in my lower legs that sees me hobble out of bed, to the lounge room, fetch a cup of tea, and take some deep breaths on the couch as I motivate myself for another twelve kilometres before sunrise.

The stairs out of my unit and down to the street are taken one at a time as I clutch the handrail in case one of my knees or hamstrings gives way. I land on each foot lightly, letting the pressure of the concrete beneath them remind my toes of what's to come for the day.

I focus intently for the first few kilometres. I assure myself with every cold step that I'll begin to feel better soon, and if I'm not warmed up by the time I get over the Miami hill, then I can always stop and walk home. I know it won't happen; the few kilometres between my Mermaid Beach unit and Miami are just enough to get my legs warmed up and find my feet. Once I get to Miami at around 5.30am, there are a few more bodies joining the path, all rugged up and taking their first steps. While I don't feel the pressure to impress them, there is always a welcome pressure that comes with onlookers around. A welcome sense of accountability and a push from a stranger running nearby, or metres behind you on the path. By the time I get to that section of path, with onlookers, with a couple of kilometres on the legs, I'm warmed up, and know that I can tackle the next ten, and run twelve kilometres before my morning coffee.

Today's blisters aren't getting better with every step. Carefully strapped and padded and tucked inside my shoes, the sensation doesn't feel better at all after trying a warm-up. There's more pressure on my feet now that they're wrapped and cushioned, and with each step, the blister burns and firmly presses against it, as though I'm not just irritating the damage, but also adding to it. After making the tough call to not run, although my energy, hydration and nutrition levels are all feeling good, I return to the balcony to remove my shoes and give my feet some elevated airtime.

I carefully peel my socks away from the blister tape. Once my socks are off, I examine all the strategically placed tape and cushioning and feel defeated as I begin to remove it all. I'd spent the best part of twenty precious minutes cutting the perfect length of tape to wrap each hotspot on my toes, then cutting pillow-like pieces of foam to place around the large, pus-filled bubbles on the inside of my feet. It was all delicately and meticulously placed to ensure each bandage wouldn't create another blister or point of pressure within my shoe. Removing it all seems such a waste.

As I expose all the left foot to fresh air, I know it's the right thing to do. It's as though the crisp, fresh air is gently kissing the oozing wounds. I then begin to unwrap the largest bandage on my right foot, one that I'd even spent $8 on getting a special blister plaster for. I carefully peel it away, unused, in the hopes I'll be able to reapply it tomorrow.

As I begin peeling off the specifically designed blister dressing, a rush overcomes me to have my feet free and elevated for the day. Guilt-free, having decided once and for all, I won't be running any further that day. At only 1pm, with the whole afternoon ahead of me, I quickly remove the last of the tape that's attached to the expensive dressing on my foot. As I do, my attention is drawn sharply from my daydreams back to my foot, where I feel a piercing pain. As I look at my precious feet, white, suffocated and soft skin is interrupted by a deep red wound. I'd just recklessly ripped the largest blister. Not only had the pus-filled balloon popped, but I'd taken some undamaged skin off my foot along with the tape.

"You idiot," I scream to myself. "Stupid idiot!"

As I dab the falling blood from my foot, I try to examine the damage I've inflicted upon myself. I fold my foot as much as I can to my face, feeling the tension of my leg muscles as I do. I stare and stare at the raw piece of my right foot that had only seconds ago been fine, protected by weathered and tough skin. I examine the raw flesh and feel its throb as air touches parts of my body that've never been exposed before.

As I stare and dab the blood away, tears begin to well in my eyes, and anger fills my throat. I'm so frustrated with myself. I had just spent an hour in preparation for another run. I'd ensured I'd eaten, and given that time to digest, I'd drank some electrolytes, done another load of washing to ensure I had running clothes for the morning. I'd gotten dressed again and I'd meticulously wrapped my feet, then in a split second, as my mind wandered to all the possibilities that lay ahead for the afternoon after deciding not to run, I'd damaged myself. The most important part of my body now. My feet, my precious feet that have now run one hundred and twenty-six kilometres over just nine days.

It was an accident. I try and bring perspective into play, but I can't shake how frustrated I was. All I needed to focus on over these thirty days was ensuring my body could run as much as possible; that's all. Everything else can wait. The actual running part, at times, seemed the easiest part. It was the preparation and everything else that was getting to me. I truly feel like the body and mind part is the easiest to wrangle if they're left undistracted. If it's just my body and mind out there running, then it's easy. It's one foot in front of the other and nothing else. But when my tired mind has to drive in a city that doesn't know how to merge, or shop at a supermarket full of dithery old people not moving

THE ART OF ~~LIVING~~ GIVING | 187

at my pace, then my mind begins to struggle.

♥

I quietly dress myself in the dim light of my bedroom lamp. Clean running clothes are lying somewhat tidy on the floor, as they're on such a high rotation. On day sixteen of running to raise awareness for mental illness, I've gathered that there's no point in putting the clothes away entirely. I know I should do another load of washing so that I have my best running shorts and bra to run tomorrow morning. I need to look after the epic heat rash that is red and raw in an exact outline of where my sports bra sits beneath my boobs. I wondered if the rash's job was to distract me from the blisters, which now no longer need bandaging to extreme lengths, and have been getting much better since I was encouraged to get proper running socks from one of the fundraiser's followers, now publicly known as #KDOGONTHEJOG.

Another #KDOGONTHEJOG supporter had paid to keep the running woman running by gifting me a massage and sending me a link to some Injinji toe socks to aid my feet to breathe and reduce the risk of blisters. I had never known running socks were a thing. I still don't feel like a runner. But as I thread my toes into their positions, I realise that two hundred and fifty kilometres in just fifteen days is a lot. Probably more than many actual runners have done in the last fifteen days.

With my toes all wrapped up in new science socks, I take my first very calculated steps of the day. I figure the slower I take them, the quicker my body will adjust to another demanding day on every muscle in my body, particularly the brain. My knees are talking the loudest of all the lower limbs, and I keep a hold of the hallway wall to assist me to the kitchen. I boil the kettle for a tea and fumble my way to the fridge. I used to be someone who didn't need to eat before a run. But lately, I've become attuned to a specific feeling that hits around the nine-kilometre mark: my body still feels strong, like it could keep going, but my eyes start to blur, and my mind gets hazy — as if I'm waking up all over again. A little bit of yoghurt and salted nuts has been enough to really carry me through those last kilometres of my morning run, and until breakfast. Even if eating at 4am is the last thing I want to do, it's proven beneficial for a few days now.

As I reach for the yoghurt, I glance at the oddly prepared plate of snacks of leftover food that Hannah has obviously rustled up the night before. She's often home from her day as a GP long after I've crawled into bed, and if she's not working late, she's studying into the ugly hours of the night for her upcoming exam. As a type 1 diabetic, Hannah's food choices are random, as they're not quite choices; they are the need for her to get in sugar, and fast.

I reach for the yoghurt and carefully thread it around the rest of our fridge contents, dodging Hannah's oddly formed snack plate. As I go to place the container of yoghurt on the bench, it never makes it. Somehow, in a split second, the yoghurt has fallen from my sure grip to the ground, making a mess and noise. I'm most concerned about the sound and disturbing Hannah from her sleep.

I've never known anyone to hate waking up as much as Hannah. It took me several months of living with her to completely understand that I had done nothing wrong and she wasn't angry at me, having only just risen from her slumber. Hannah's hate for mornings actually encouraged my love for mornings as I would sooner be outside running, watching the sunrise or sitting at the local cafe than be at home in the firing line. On the polar opposite end of me, and my lack of want for food getting straight out of bed, it's up there with the only reason she will get out of bed. Her first action was to take a direct route to the kitchen to put some bread in the toaster, so she could eat as soon as possible.

As I'm folded over, cleaning the last of the yoghurt from the floor, I feel the tug of my hamstrings, reminding me of how many kilometres I've done, and forcing me to assess how many I hope to do today. I carefully wiggle my hips around in the kitchen as I prepare my small serving of yoghurt by scraping down the last of the tub's contents. As I do, I realise I'll need to buy more today and feel instantly frustrated again for having dropped the container in the first place, losing yoghurt to the kitchen floor, which amounts to another job on my list for the day, that isn't just running. I think back to the moment I dropped it and can't even understand how it happened. It's not as though I had a loose grip or felt it precariously clutched within my hand. It was in my hand one second and on the floor the next. As I relive the moment over again, the pain in my legs reminds me once more of what I've achieved in the last sixteen days. If this body has done an unusual amount of running and food prepping, and washing, then isn't it fair to drop just one yoghurt container?

Quietly and carefully, I pour the boiling water over my lemon & ginger tea bag. I calculate my movements as I clutch carefully at my small yoghurt bowl and head towards the lounge to fuel up. My legs rejoice as I find my spot on the couch, and begin to melt away, just as I realise I've forgotten to get myself a spoon.

I begin to bargain with myself about how getting up right now means I'll get to eat sooner and feel the energy creep in sooner on my run. I spring from the couch before my legs bargain against my brain. I decide not to journey an additional one and a half metres around into the kitchen, instead deciding to reach over the counter and into the top drawer for a spoon. I gently touch the drawer's contents to determine which utensils I can feel, and decide I'll opt for a dessert spoon, as they're more in reach than the teaspoons. Grabbing it, I begin to straighten myself up from over the counter until I hear a loud clang. Looking intently at my empty hands, I examine in increasing anger just how the spoon has left my hold. First, the yoghurt and now the spoon. *Poor Hannah.* I drag myself into the kitchen, realising I should have just done so in the first place. I pick up the spoon, and though I think it would no doubt be fine to eat off, I don't dare take the risk and have the one thing that stops me running be some kind of germ I picked up off our kitchen floor.

17

Surprised by how much energy I have, I pull open my laptop to pen an update to everyone who has pledged their support for #KDOGONTHEJOG.

'Hello to the lot of you dear pledging legends,

I would like to start by officially saying thank you from the bottom of my heart. With your pledges and my current kilometres, I've reached 280 clicks in 16 days. I have already achieved my goal of raising $4,000 for many wonderful mental health services. I am currently running at a rate of $22.10 per kilometre, so that is now $6,188 in pledged donations - Whacky Doo!

I really should have constructed this email prior to running 35 kilometres today, but I've learnt to realise that my prioritising capabilities are something that subsides in my exhaustion.

I suppose I just wanted to check in and let you all know how I'm going. Not all of the wonderful pledgers are on Instagram, and even if you are, I'm not sure you've been able to see the sheer amount of sh*t I have dropped in the last few days. Literally, the last few days were a real push. I physically dropped so many things. My poor housemate Hannah is leading up to a really big exam (she's spent every waking minute studying for the last 4 months), and I'm over here at 4 am dropping my yoghurt over the floor, dropping spoons, I've got drink bottles leaping from my hands, letting doors slam shut – you name it, I've dropped it. I was wondering for a bit there if it was exhaustion or just my calves screaming for a quick stretch on the regular... like "Hey, drop this so you have to bend down and stretch me whilst ya pick that thing up!"

The dropping thing has definitely been an external display of what was (or wasn't) going on in my head. The previous few days have been very blurry. I set off on this mission with the sheer intention of doing a good thing, honouring my beautiful cousin, honouring the hardships of those struggling with mental illness, tipping my own hat to my mental health, raising awareness, raising conversation, etc. I really didn't think things through much further than that. I knew I had the determination, but I really didn't know I had this much, nor did I realise it would be this hard, and I definitely didn't know just how much grit this girl has in her. The hard bit isn't necessarily the running. The hard bit is the amount of food I'm having to eat, the loads of washing I'm having to do, the constant dressing and un-dressing of blisters, the putting oneself down for a nap, the food prep, the liquid consumption, the stretching, the looming house chores that make me feel like crap... pretty much everything that life includes outside of when the runners are on.

I've learnt to cut myself lots of slack. Don't tell my mother, but the active wear gets washed, dried and then is laid across the floor at the foot of my bed... because why fold and put it away if it's going to be worn again in less than 48 hours?

Anyway, what I'm here to actually say... and you might have already gathered from the above... is that I've been very lost in my head and own endeavours, that I've forgotten why I'm really here... and what I'm really doing. I am simply here to raise a bit of chatter, raise some awareness and hopefully raise some funds for some of these lifesaving organisations. That's the real powerful thing about this whole fundraiser, and these mental health organisations. You just don't have any idea what impact you are making. It's not like there's a qualitative value in just what your contribution is doing. There is no telling just which conversation, or which call to any of these services, is saving lives, or perhaps has already saved a life.

I managed to hold onto that thought today and began to find my groove again. I accepted that it is equally important to be selfless and selfish, always, in whatever you are doing. I've had a few selfish days, where I had to look after my own feet, my own tummy and my own head, but that is arguably the most important thing we can do. I should not feel guilty for forgetting why I'm running, because all we are ever responsible for is ourselves, our own actions, and our own thoughts.

So I encourage you to somehow check in with yourself, gather up the courage to have the difficult conversations with yourself, because that is most often the hardest conversation; some don't even know where to begin with talking to others, because they are yet to really get to know themselves.

Running 280km is a good way to have a chat with yourself, I'll tell ya that much.

Anyway, more from me later, when I feel it's due.

Thanks again, you are absolutely wonderful, xo.'

♥

As I gently close the lid of our top-loader washing machine at 7am and quickly turn the loud dial to the 'soak' setting, I remind myself of the earlier advice I'd penned to my followers. *It's equally important to be selfish and selfless. And selfishly, the heat rash around my boobs really needs its best ventilation for another run later today, so these clothes really need to be washed, regardless of Hannah still being asleep.*

I feel less guilty about possibly disturbing her when I reach the kitchen after finding a pile of her dishes from last night hasn't been actioned, only added to. I've been able to find forgiveness for these things regularly, as she's studying around the clock. *Surely she can forgive me for really needing clothes washed when I'm running around the clock?*

I carefully untangle our best fry pan from the pile of dirty dishes and clean it in the sink. Unsure of what was previously cooked in there, I question the stickiness of whatever is left behind and wonder what on earth it could be. *I hope Hannah is never cooking that again.* I place the loosely dried pan over the flame and allow the heat to dry out the rest. I open the fridge and stare blankly at its ingredients, trying to focus on my shelf, yet distracted by another teetering plate of random half-eaten pieces of fruit and slabs of cheese. The visual of the brown, uncovered and partially rotting avocado manages to zap me of any inkling of hunger, yet I know I need to eat. I struggle to remember what I was planning to prepare, now that I've been distracted by dishes and my flatmates' questionable food storage choices. *Eggs. I'm having some eggs for breakfast.* Although I'm not overly hungry, I need to eat something filling and filling myself with a high-protein breakfast should hopefully keep me sustained for my morning shift and help my achy muscles repair themselves. I consider any other protein-rich options, and the only other option is a protein shake. It's exactly what I feel like, something I can just sip at and slowly digest over the next hour or so, or even on my drive to work. But I wouldn't dare fire up the blender in addition to the washing machine. I wonder for a moment if I have time to wait a little while longer, in the hopes that Hannah wakes up, then maybe I can make the breakfast I really want to eat. I consider my options and decide I'd prefer to just eat eggs now in silence, and without having to navigate the inevitable guilt I will feel as I tiptoe around a not-so-freshly risen Hannah. *Eggs will be fine, I'll just make some eggs.*

As I push my way through the bowl of scrambled eggs, an unsettling discomfort creeps in. As another unwanted meal navigates its way to my belly, I begin to feel queasy, questioning why I even chose the eggs. *I ate the eggs because it was the quietest option.* I ate the eggs out of consideration for my sleeping housemate. But this morning, as eggs begin to turn in my stomach, I'm realising how unfair that is.

I've run three hundred and fifty kilometres in the past twenty days, yet I'm neglecting the very body that has relentlessly carried me through every demand. That's not fair. I check my phone and see that it's 7.50am. This body woke at 4am, long before it wanted to. It unwillingly had some mouthfuls of yoghurt and nuts, long before its digestive system had started for the day. It endured the searing pain of a razor-like bra digging into raw flesh, forced undesirable shoes onto wounded feet, stretched fatigued legs and hips that begged for rest, carried me step after step for twelve kilometres, and sipped black coffee to save a buck. And yet, I denied it the protein smoothie it craved. *That's not fair.*

As I force down another bite of eggs, I bargain with myself. *These will fuel me through the morning and make me feel good.* Yet as I chew, the waves of turmoil begin to change into waves of total appreciation and gratitude for everything this body and I have accomplished together. Pride swells as I empty the bowl, a genuine sense of appreciation replacing discomfort. The realisation ignites a fierce determination to start prioritising this incredible body, no matter the noise or disruption it might cause.

It's been years and years of living with other people, always placing myself second. I cared for Jake, then for Anna and now, although I'm not having to shower or dress Hannah, I'm still putting her needs before my own. *This has to stop. Perhaps the next chapter is to live alone on my own schedule and at my own pace. A life where I can blend smoothies whenever I want.*

♥

As I carefully climb the stairs of our Mermaid Beach unit, I'm excited to see a lovely big peace lily, wrapped in decoration, sitting at our doorstep. I'm confident today, of all the days that I've ever lived, that the gift must be for me. I have run four hundred and ninety-five kilometres over the last thirty days and have just five more to run today before I celebrate with anyone available for a beer. It's been one whole year since the world lost Ashley. This beautiful gift must be for me.

My hips allow for a deep squat as I pick up the plant from the doormat. It's big and healthy, and my mind immediately wonders who would've sent them. It must be someone who's not around or able to come and congratulate me as I finish this afternoon's run. But who? I excitedly unlocked our front door with one hand, the plant lovingly embraced by the other, propped on my hip like a child. Once I get inside, I place the large gift down on our dining table and read the words on the card. The urge to read the bottom line first, to know the sender, is quickly relieved by the first line.

'To our beautiful daughter Karlee.
An amazing effort! We are so very proud of you!
With love, Mum and Dad xoxo'

I read the words repeatedly, feeling the swell of pride rise within me, too. I wonder what exactly my parents are most proud of. Was it the fact that I've run this many kilometres with no proper running experience, having just upgraded from the netball shoes I've had since I was thirteen? Was it because I set an ambitious goal and nurtured every part of myself to achieve it? Or perhaps it's the fact that I single-handedly campaigned to raise nearly $15,000 for mental health charities.

Perhaps their pride stems from witnessing the past thirty days. The deeply meaningful tribute I made in memory of my cousin, their nephew. But part of me wonders if their pride runs deeper, tied to their daughter's quiet transformation. The daughter who just eight months ago struggled to find a reason to get out of bed now rises each day with purpose at 4am to lace up her boots and take on the world.

Maybe they're proud of the choices I've made over the past eight months. The time spent going inwards. The decision to step back and work only twelve hours a week allowed me to sit in this unit by the beach and rediscover who I really am and what I truly wanted from life. Maybe it's the fact that, no matter how ugly things got, I just kept going. I watched every sunrise and built connections with my community. I poured my heart and mind into creating a business, a business that will soon see the light of day. In a chapter in my life that felt overwhelmingly lonely and isolating, I refused to stand still. I took action over and over again. No playing the victim, no comparisons to others, no blame poking at those who had broken my heart. I simply kept moving forward. One foot in front of the other, through blisters, heartbreak, and heat rash. Perhaps that's what my parents are most proud of. That their daughter found strength in struggle, purpose in pain, and the courage to keep showing up no matter what.

♥

"Do you have time to make me a sandwich for lunch today, Karls?" Harry politely asks as I meet him out on his balcony, overlooking Elanora Lake.

"Of course I do! I've got plenty of time, Harry!" I assured him, with still twenty-five minutes left of my shift.

"Some ham and salad?" I suggest.

THE ART OF ~~LIVING~~ GIVING

"Yeah! That sounds lovely. Whatever you can muster up there would be good, young lady. I just don't want Catherine to do a thing today. She's right into it all out there in her studio, so I don't want to keep her from the creative flow," he explains kindly.

"Oh, good on her! Not a problem, I'll go and prep something for you now."

I wander back up the ramp. It was carefully designed to suit the house and installed after Harry had his fall from a ladder a little over five years ago, just as he and Catherine entered retirement. Their home is adorned with lamps, large plants, and a variety of different sitting areas featuring eclectic pieces of furniture. At the heart of the home is Catherine's kitchen, a lover of food and keeping herself and her family fed on the very best ingredients, collected every Saturday at the Palm Beach farmer's market. The week's meals are planned after great thought and consideration for the seasonal produce that's available. Equipped with her lists, hat, and reusable shopping bags, off she treks early each Saturday morning, often before I've arrived to get Harry showered and dressed for his day. No matter what time she returns, whether I've just wheeled Harry out of the shower dripping wet, or he's laid on the bed as I'm securing his catheter bag for the day, at the sound of the garage door, he insists I stop whatever I'm doing, to go and assist her in bringing in her bags - and I gladly do. It's in these moments that I know his disability hinders him the most. He's left his pride long behind and can gratuitously accept the help of a paid employee showering or dressing him, but his inability to assist his wife in holding the door or carrying bags is what hurts him the most.

I enjoy it whenever Harry asks me to prepare food for him.

I know my cooking would never stack up to Catherine's and, even if it did, I know he was a gentleman long before he was a husband, so he would never declare anyone's food to be better than his wife's. There's no pressure preparing food for him, but there is a joy in pulling the finest ingredients from the clean and tidy fridge.

I fill today's freshly baked loaf of homemade bread with the finest leg ham off the bone from the local butcher, some organic lettuce that has already been washed, and kept with a layer of paper towel within a Tupperware container in the crisper, some beetroot, pickled onions that Catherine has prepared herself, and a perfect tomato from the large ceramic fruit bowl that sits atop the bench - looking like a piece of art, the bowl was hand built and painted by Catherine for this purpose.

I thoughtfully filled the sandwich with just enough filling so that it remains within the bread slices, allowing Harry to handle it with his compromised hand function. I place it on a plate and cover it with Gladwrap, leaving the edges loose enough to unwrap easily. I rearrange some of the other ingredients in the fridge to ensure the plate is left at an accessible height for Harry.

Having cleaned down the chopping board and put away all the ingredients, I scan the kitchen before heading back out to Harry. His eyes are heavy, and he's taking long blinks that break his stare across the lake.

"Coffee?" I promote, as part of the usual last step of my shift.
"Would you mind?" He asks.
"Not at all!" I assure him, almost annoyed with his pleasantry.

I pop back inside and prepare his coffee; two long shots over a dash of Bonsoy milk, that's been microwaved for twenty seconds in one of Catherine's hand-built ceramic mugs, the one with a blue chicken on it - my personal favourite. As I wait for the last pod to pour into his mug, I watch Harry transfer from his mechanical wheelchair to the table and chairs that fit only him and Catherine, where they enjoy breakfast and coffee while watching over the lake.

"Here you are, young man," I tease, placing the mug near his strong hand.

"Why, thank you!" He says with joy. "What's on for the rest of the day?"

"Oh well, I've got some orders to pack, then off to the post office," I explain.

"Having a wine at the beach tonight?" Harry wonders in awe at my evening ritual.

"You bet! There's been some cracking sunsets the last couple of nights. I can't wait!" I declare.

"Ah, good on ya. Well, go and enjoy yourself, young lady!"

"Thank you! And I'll let you know if I see any better post bags at the post office…" I begin to explain before Harry interrupts.

"No, it's alright. Don't worry about them. I'll order them. You don't need to go to extra effort to find those bags." He says it as though I'm moving heaven and earth for him.

"Harry, it's seriously no trouble. I'll already be at the post office," I confirm.

"Oh, I know, but it's not necessary if I can just have them shipped here. That's easy. Now get outta here and don't think about me or the post bags for another second!"

"Alright then. Well, I'll see you in the morning!" I say, making a turn to head up the ramp.

"See ya then!" he calls.

I walk out the door after singing out my farewells to Catherine. Her hands are busy, covered in clay. As I climb into the car at 11.15am, I'm the most relaxed I've been in some time. I ponder back over Harry's wishes not to have me thinking about his post bags or him, which I confirm is the very best part of the job. Harry is a pleasure to care for because of his emotional intelligence and selflessness. I struggle to fathom Harry in the inevitable darkness that he had to endure after his accident. His positive attitude toward his disability is something I've not witnessed in caring for Anna or Aiden, and I think it's among the best attitudes of anyone I've ever met, with or without a disability. I wonder how the struggle changes having a disability later in life, and naturally compare the likes of Aiden, who was born with his disability and never knew life walking, compared to Harry, who lived a full life on his own two feet, and had to adjust in later years of life. Both unimaginable traumas, but one thing I know Harry has come to terms with is his ability to ask for and accept help, without any destruction to his ego. While inevitably crushing, not having the independence or ability to do as he pleases, he lets that go the moment it raises its ugly head. Letting it go seems far less tiring, and you can hear Harry's lightness whenever you're in earshot as he sits on his balcony overlooking the lake. He hums and sings and talks to all the water dragons that also call Harry and Catherine's beautiful garden home. I've rarely seen Harry get hung up on his shitty hand; to him, there's no point. He accepts the cards, asks for the help of others to deal with it, then quickly moves on, allowing his energy to move through with each passing moment. Harry cherishes his own peace so fiercely that he's accepted asking for help from others, which allows him to move on more quickly.

As I turn the key in the ignition, I let my thoughts drift away from Harry, just as he had hoped. It's quite effortless, knowing that he's out on his balcony, humming softly, with a coffee in hand. His lightness of being seems almost contagious, and I begin to wonder how I'll spend the rest of my day. It's not even midday yet, and I've accomplished so much. Rising before sunrise, reading, meditating, running five kilometres, savouring moments at my local cafe, and now, wrapping up work for the day without a hint of stress. All of this, thanks to a gentleman who has embraced receiving help with such grace that neither shame nor burden clouds his life-or mine.

18

It's been two months since I completed #KDOGONTHEJOG. Possibly one of the greatest physical and mental feats I'd ever endure. I stare at the skinny hands that hold my phone as I scroll through Instagram. The wrists that have been pressing my body away from the floor, at least ten times a day, since I stopped running. Now I've given my body permission to not run every day, and only run when I want to, I've found I miss the feeling of achieving and conquering something new. The satisfaction each day I had running, as the lengths became easier, and the fact that I'd done it the day prior proved I could turn around and do it again. That was satisfaction unlike anything else. The constant improvement and self-mastery were quickly something I missed once the thirty days had come to an end. Not to mention, there was also a following of a financial figure that kept growing each day.

THE ART OF ~~LIVING~~ GIVING | 205

So, with the absence of building up to something or building on top of, I decided to master just ten push-ups. My lower body felt strong and nimble, yet my upper body has never been a strong point. So, now every morning, following my big running feat, I still rise with time to greet the day before most do in Mermaid Beach. I carry myself along the beach at a pace that feels comfortable for the day. Sometimes I run, sometimes I just walk. Then, after I sit at table 36 at BSKT cafe, where I have sat now for nearly a year, having conversations with fellow early birds, forming friendships with the staff and enjoying my coffee, I return to my beachside unit and do ten push-ups. Recording them on my phone to track my progress over time and to watch as my core becomes closer to the floor as I master such a simple thing. I've watched these wrists, the same ones that hold my phone, become less and less buckled under the pressure of my body as I watch them hold the pushups in recent videos. I marvel at the resilience of my body and the human body generally. I look at dark freckles atop my pointer finger that grew from getting badly burnt as I trekked the Himalayas as a young teen. The same hands that have pumped life back into the chest of a loved one. The hands that held Jake's hands for hours on end as he recovered from his latest ordeal. The hands that string tunes on a guitar and hold schooners at the pubs with mates. The hands that grab at anything I tell them to, and today, comfortable and happy, I can't help but marvel at the change and how pleasantly unfamiliar the bony little wrist bones look.

I direct my gaze back to my phone and continue scrolling through Instagram. As I move further through the feed, I'm stopped by one picture. A woman adorned in loud running gear, with a big smile, as she climbed a red dirt track. I could instantly tell from the shade of the red rock and starkness, and the heat that it was taken in central Australia. There was something about central Australia that fascinated me, especially the thought of walking its trails for days. I think it was because of how familiar I'd become with the high country of Victoria as a young adventurer. The vegetation and landscape had become so familiar. While I wasn't good at absorbing the names of plants or trees, I'd spent hours lost in examining single leaves or the colours of rock beneath my feet as I walked for hours on end. I'd learnt a lot about nature and myself on those trails as a young kid, and there was something about the stark difference of the red rock of central Australia that had always pulled me to want to walk them. In later years, many of the friends I'd made at Wollangarra took career paths in outdoor education or similar fields, and I'd now witnessed a few of them lead hikes on the Larapinta Trail.

As I stared at the woman undertaking the red rugged path, I knew it had to be the Larapinta Trail. I just didn't know people run it. I change my line of sight from the details in the picture to the caption beneath it. The caption explains that the company is in its final days of signups for 'Run Larapinta.' I continue reading the caption, captivated and with an unexpected pull and urge to do it. As I review the information, I know I need the date to be far enough away to prepare myself, yet not too far away that I spend too much time training for it.

April 21st 2021. Four months away. The information lands well. It feels close enough to keep this current momentum going, to continue flowing with my running, yet not too far in the future, because there's still a voice somewhere within questioning if running is suited to me and my aching hips. I refer to the website for more information and read about the words like 'rugged,' 'agonising,' and 'scrambling,' and with every frightful word, I become more eager to witness this sacred stretch of Australia's outback, with just myself, and this body that accepts wild challenges.

As I continue to read the traversing terrain, I understand there would be a need for training, which excites me. I've never trained as a runner before. Sure, I've bought myself some good active wear, a pair of Injini socks and upgraded my runners, and run as much as my little legs could handle in thirty days. But I still didn't consider myself a runner. A runner would follow a program and train on different terrains at calculated lengths to ensure they build their strength. They wouldn't just run from Mermaid Beach to Tallebudgera Creek and back every day.

As I continue my evaluation and become more convinced that I need to sign up, I see a link to a training guide for the run. The training almost seemed more exciting than the four-day running event itself. I open the manual to see if I have enough time to prepare. As I count back the weeks from April 21st, I discover that this week is the second week of that training schedule. *I'm only a week behind.* It's the final urge I need.

Before my small savings account, which was longing to launch Seed A Smile, had any influence in the decision, I input my credit card details and paid $797. I'm doing it. I will train hard and properly for the next four months before I run four days across the Larapinta Trail. *I'm doing it for me this time. No fundraisers, and no one following the process. Just for me to enjoy. For Karlee, who will wake early and work hard to juggle her nutrition, care for her body and have the pleasure of another epic accomplishment.* I know there's part of this that's torture. And now that the funds have left my account, I feel the demands of running begin to clutch at my legs. I feel the memory of careful steps of a morning as I wait for my legs to warm up, hobbling to the kitchen, just longing for my legs to warm up again. I begin to worry as I fathom that these same legs, which have successfully held me running for thirty days straight, may not be able to handle four months of training. *I guess there's only one way to find out.*

♥

I feel the literal load of my body lift as I sit on the sun-drenched balcony chair of the apartment I'm staying at in Penguin, Tasmania. My legs are ready to enjoy some elevation time after just completing a trail run as part of my week six training run in the nearby national parks. Feeling the air kiss my toes, and the sun soak my freshly showered face, I sip some water to try to replenish my fluids and prepare myself for a glass of Tassie red. *Things couldn't really be sweeter.* I still have the whole afternoon to enjoy here on this sunny balcony, and I've just been to the local grocery store, a family-run IGA, and stocked up on the finest of Tasmanian produce. It feels like the first time I've really stopped after a busy December, when I finished working for Aiden and have now accepted more consistent shifts with Harry, including Saturday and Sunday mornings, which financially top me up to a comfortable weekly wage. Leaving Aiden's care team was a difficult decision, one that I knew would break his heart, and didn't come without his begging and guilt-tripping, as well as promises of a higher hourly rate. But it was necessary for my sanity. I felt so sorry for him and do feel like he was becoming a better person from my influence (sometimes), but my heart broke most because he didn't have any family or true friends he could rely on. I felt that was something we all deserved, yet it's evident that his lack of support was for a reason - the same reason I needed to leave his team. I got to enjoy Christmas in Victoria, even though it looked unlikely to happen with QLD's borders only just opening up after the pandemic. I ran the hills where I grew up, as I juggled my training with enjoying a lot of Mum's cooking, and dabbling in some drinks. I journeyed back to the Gold Coast for a fleeting night back in my little unit, before driving myself, Harry and Catherine up to Brisbane Airport for an early morning flight to Hobart on the first day of 2021.

This was my first big interstate trip with them and, so far, it seems like an opportunity few would ever be lucky to call 'work.' We will be in Tasmania for the next six weeks to avoid the peak of the Gold Coast humidity and ultimately protect Harry from overheating. The gig for me means I get to have a welcome and paid change of pace. The most enjoyable part is that no part of this is a chore. It's an actual joy to pop around to Harry and Catherine's accessible beachside apartment in the morning and help Harry get showered and dressed, before we part ways for the day. Financially, this trip is also beneficial enough that I decided to sell my car just before leaving and buy a van upon my return.

The last few days felt busy in transit and travelling north to the small town of Penguin on the North coast of Tasmania. But today was a better pace. Both Catherine and Harry and I have settled into our accommodation, and navigating the second shower there at Harry's accommodation was easier the second time around. I left them to their day at just 10am, then borrowed the hire car to head for the nearby hills to continue my training for the Larapinta.

As I sit recovering, I feel each breath finding a deeper place in my lungs, and my heart rate settling. I consciously scan my body for any tension, and the last muscles I feel relax are the ones around my jaw. As I open my mouth to stretch the tight muscles, I'm reminded of the mouthful of ulcers I had endured this time, only twelve months ago. I begin to recount the entire state I was in. The job caring for Anna, my aching head and generally the lack of life that sat within my grieving body. As I move my jaw again, in an attempt to relax the muscles that have become accustomed to being tight due to stress, I recount in awe all that I have achieved in the last 12 months. As I do, it's as though I feel time slow down. Here on this sunny balcony, with nowhere else to be, it's as though my heart is at genuine rest. There's not a single stress that clutches onto any part of me or my body. To hold onto whatever ingredients have made this moment and this feeling, I recount what has occurred today. I woke early in my own space and on my own watch.

Unknowingly, I followed my old morning ritual! I woke early, without fearing I'd wake or disturb anyone. I made a cup of coffee loudly, jumped back into bed with my book, and ensured I read my handmade bookmark that hosted the words of the same affirmation I'd recounted since 2017, when I first started the routine. Once I finished my coffee, I took to the floor for 10 push-ups and a stretch, then lay flat on my back to breathe deeply and focus my attention in silence. Then, once I'd eaten that delicious toast with fresh tomato and Tasmania's rich duck river butter, I wandered down to my friends Harry and Catherine. Harry and I chatted away, as we did most of the time we'd spent together, then after he was all ready for his day, I went for a long trail run. I think it must be a combination of all of that that has me feeling so good. On track, on time, and exactly where I should be. The training program is another reminder that I'm exactly where I should be to get to where I want to go. All that I can achieve now on these legs is exactly what I'll need to carry me across the outback for four days.

Having now sipped my way through another litre of water, I give myself permission to crack open the bottle of chilling pinot noir and drink in the rest of the afternoon, as one happy, contented, fit and peace-filled woman. *I'm exactly where I'm meant to be.*

19

"So I'm really never going to see you ever again?" Tim, the sweet, dreadlocked boy whom I only met yesterday afternoon, asks. I slide on my shoes in the early hours of the morning in his Hobart hotel room. I'm pleased I have my back to him, as I don't know what facial expressions would be across my face.

"Well, who knows! Never say never!" I tease, finding my handbag and preparing to leave. As my eyes struggle to make out its contents, I feel the strain of my head. We met at a pub in Salamanca early the prior afternoon, and after getting excited by each other's company, we jumped from pub to pub and from one topic of conversation to the next. We had chatted like old friends reunited. I smile to myself and look for my Airbnb house keys. *I wonder how many beers we actually drank?*

My head feels heavy and my eyesight blurry, but I'm shocked I actually don't feel that hungover. I'm light and carefree, unlike any recent memory of the morning after many drinks. Still searching for my keys, I ponder the real science of hangovers and how much nice company plays a part in how well you wake up the next day.

"We can hang out again, at least?" Tim asks again casually, as he grapples that I'm about to walk out of his hotel and life.

"I don't know. I have my brother and his family arriving today. I can hardly be sneaking around for catch-ups with a guy I've just met! It's really not me at all," I explain as I search the nearby bedside table for my keys.

"Ah! Idiot," I declare abruptly.

"What? Me?" Tim asks timidly.

"No, Me!" I declare as I spring to my feet. "I don't have the keys. They're in the keybox," I explain with a hint of embarrassment.

I turn to look at Tim, still lying in bed, ready to sleep off more of the morning. *Is this really the last time I'll see him?* He's not from Hobart; he's here training before he boards the ship to Antarctica, where he's employed to live and work as a carpenter for a year. This had been a cool thing to converse over initially, but it was the least fascinating thing about him. I think back to the afternoon prior and remember the moment I felt like I'd met him before. I'd spent the first hour trying to figure out who he reminded me of. I had watched his lips move as he spoke of his home in Taree, a place I'd never been, and his recent years travelling. I'd watch his delicate and doll-like face move as he nervously spun stories, and with each furrow of his brows, or each sparkle of humour, I wondered how I'd known him.

I listened to his stories, waiting for the one that would explain our paths having crossed, but as the night went on, we went from just two strangers who shouted one another a beer at the first pub, then declared we'd be interested in moving to another, then another. As the night grew on, I began to accept that I'd never met him. Rather, he was just familiar. His presence feels as though I'm catching up with one of the boys I went through primary and high school with. Drinking beers with Tim had felt like I was merely catching up on time away from a friend. I had thought originally, we were hitting it off, but as his familiarity grew, and the likened feeling of him being an old friend, I'd assumed that he would politely tell me he was heading home alone at some point.

The night got rowdier as we landed in the only pub still open. The courtyard was filled with very intoxicated people, predominantly men. It was there, when I got accidentally shoved into on my way back from the bathroom by a drunken bloke, that Tim quickly came to my side, asking if I fancied leaving. I was somewhat disappointed, as I had figured this would be the point at which we part ways. But as we'd walked out the front of the pub, Tim carefully and calculatedly mentioned having some beers in his hotel room that we could go to, or he could go get the beers, and we could drink by the water. I knew at this point that he, too, didn't know if we were just two strangers who had become good friends in one night, or if there was a little more interest than that. I'd assured him that I was happy to go back to his hotel. Shortly after that, Tim reached for my hand. The lightness that followed for both of us was childlike. I swung our arms playfully, making us both laugh, and as we exchanged glances, Tim looked at me and leaned in for a kiss, in the middle of Parliament House Gardens in Hobart.

Now, I'm possibly walking out of his hotel room and never seeing him again. I grapple with the thought as I take a seat on the edge of the bed, ready to leave. I wonder if the only reason I feel so unsure of what to do is that it's the first romantic relation I've had with anyone since Noah dumped me seven months ago. I wonder if this feeling and attraction to Tim is just because someone is paying me attention. But I can't shake the feeling of uncertainty. I can't bring myself to leave without ever seeing him again.

"Do you remember what you said last night when you were drunk?" I ask Tim with a teasing smirk on my face.

"Urgh, God, I don't know? Was it lame?" He asks.

"You said I should wait for you. And that you could see yourself falling in love with me…" I say teasingly, but genuinely wondering how much of that was true.

"Hah, kinda… I do remember you saying that you feel like we were lovers in a past life, though," he reflects.

I do remember saying that. And that makes the most sense of all these feelings that I'm grappling with right now. *That's exactly what this is. We were lovers at another time, and if I believe it or not, in a past life. But we're not meant to be lovers in this life. He's off to Antarctica and returning home to Taree. I love my life on the Gold Coast. It was pure chance that we met, and perhaps it was some kind of glitch in the simulation of life we live in. But I know that now's not our time.* Comforted by the feeling, I bounce to my feet and lean over to give Tim a goodbye kiss.

"Is this goodbye?" He asks quietly, as my lips near his. We kiss.

"Yep. I really enjoyed spending time with you. You're an incredibly beautiful person. Have the best time in Antarctica," I say as I climb back up off the bed.

"You're a beautiful person too," Tim says, deflated.

As I near the door determinedly, I feel uncertain I've done the right thing. Wanting desperately to leave and continue on my fiercely independent life that only just days ago felt like I was exactly where I was meant to be, I wonder. *What would be the harm of seeing Tim again? Surely there's no harm in exchanging details?* I let the softness in me, the part that feels as though I've just spent the night with a trusted friend, win.

"I guess we could find some time to catch up over the next two weeks?" I say just a foot away from the door. I watch as a smile takes over Tim's face.

♥

I focus intently on the feet running ahead of me, trying to stay close enough and match their strong pace. This morning, day four of Run Larapinta brings an added time pressure not experienced on the previous days. As I pick each step within the loose sand of the red riverbed, I search my line of path for any tree roots that could trip up my precious feet. My head's attention darts from the head itself right down to the searing pain beneath my right, flat foot. I lovingly gave my feet the best possible chance of making it through today's run, the last of four days, and the longest day yet. I rose even earlier this morning to watch a video my osteopath had shared with me about the best way to strap my ankles. I'd reached out to him at the end of day three, explaining the sensation that my ankles can no longer hold weight in any way. They carried me predominantly downhill on loose pebbles for the last five kilometres of the day. Each gruelling step found my ankles rolling out, rolling in; any direction dictated by the placement of the pebbles beneath my foot. My body would follow, falling over the soft ankles. I took each loose step, disgruntled, until I made another finish line. Done for the day, but unsure of how I would tackle day four. I rang my osteopath Jordy, whom I trusted with any kind of advice, be it mental or physical. He had recommended strapping my ankles for day four and had shared the video.

Having never strapped my ankles before, I set my alarm forty-five minutes earlier to allow myself the time to do it and prepare for another long day in the harsh Australian sun. My parents had come along to support me, meaning I got to sleep in a comfortable bed in their caravan, enjoy all my meals prepared for me, and have their support at the end of every long day. As I woke in the morning, I sincerely hoped that the first steps across the caravan would prove to me, like never before, just how much repair can be done in just one night's sleep. The steps don't feel good at all; my ankles are still giving way beneath the weight of my body.

I carefully cut strapping tape and meticulously place it around my ankles, perfectly following the placements explained in the video. Mum places a coffee for me among the tape and scissors, and the silence between my parents and me speaks volumes about how pained and worried we all are. I know my mum is intentionally not offering any comfort, because she knows how pained I am, and how the comfort might just push the Karlee that needs to cry into not giving the final day of running a go.

I begin to climb up out of the dry riverbed and head up into the red cliffs. Adding to the fear of day four is the time pressure of reaching checkpoint one, which is thirteen kilometres away, in under one and a half hours. It's a solid run on flat ground with fresh legs, let alone ankles that have lost all strength on their fourth day scrambling over a desert ridgeline. There's really no time to catch my breath or plod along for the morning. I need to move as quickly as possible to reach checkpoint one on time; otherwise, I might be asked to finish there and not be allowed to continue to the finish line. Unlike the other days, I only have my eyes set on checkpoint one. I'm not convinced I'll even be able to manage that without doing serious damage to my ankles.

As I climb and climb, I feel the strapping tape digging into the skin on the top of my feet. While the tape feels as though it's now cutting into my flesh, it doesn't scream louder than the slapping pain under the right foot as it lands upon the hard plastic orthotic. My ankles are so fragile, I've made the call to run with my orthotics, which I never usually do. A big no-no for any distance runner is testing their body by doing something so out of routine. The pain beneath my right foot loudly announces it has reached the four-kilometre mark this morning. I've battled for the last two kilometres with my head, wondering whether I even have the time to stop, undo my shoes, remove the orthotics, get tied up, and then get back running, or if that will jeopardise reaching checkpoint one.

I can't hear anything else or feel any other emotion than the torture of the base of my right foot. Before long, an urge stronger than anything I've felt before – even running through blisters or insane heat rash – grips so tightly it's as though my head has no say in the matter. I spot a nice flat rock, perched just off to the side of the track ahead, and as I move closer to it, I remove my vest and prepare to plant myself upon the rock and remove my shoes. The other reason I've prolonged removing the hard orthotics from my shoes was in case they were actually providing some support to my rolling ankles. Anything would be good. Not to mention prolonging the relief that would come from simply removing them from my shoes. I suspect it'll feel like such a treat that I want to savour it.

As I lace up my shoes and get moving, I feel the cushion of my trail shoe now caressing the base of my foot. *Why did it take me so long to stop and ditch the orthotics?* I knew I should have listened as my body screamed to tell me to remove them. I feel the blood returning to the tips of my toes, having not fully understood they had gone numb. I consider how dangerous that was. *I wonder if I'd taken off my sock back there, what colour my toes would have been?*

I look up ahead of me to my fellow competitors who are clambering up the red rocks to reach the top of the ridge line. I spot the khaki shirt that I had been following before, not too far ahead, and set myself the task of attempting to catch back up to him and follow his pace. It's as though the more blood that circulates to my feet, the more present I become. I start to take in the colours of the rock under the shade of the ridgeline. I realise I ought to enjoy this particular climb, as the ridgeline protects us from the lower lying morning sun. Knowing that once we're on top of this ridge, that's where we will predominantly stay for a while.

I reach to my chest, where two sleeves of electrolytes sit balanced a top of each breast pocket of my blue running vest. I feel the left first and realise it's full. I frantically feel the right and shockingly learn I've not nearly consumed anywhere near enough for this point of the run. *Have I touched any of my water?* I try to recount the last seven to nine kilometres. *I've been so caught up in the inner conflict of whether to stop and remove the orthotic that I've barely had enough to drink!*

Feeling like I've failed myself, I remember back to even earlier this morning. *I battled with all my might to hold down my breakfast on the drive to the start line, because I'd stupidly taken my anti-inflammatories as soon as I got out of bed.* That wasn't indifferent from other mornings, but rather than following that with breakfast, I'd followed that with forty-five minutes spent on strapping my ankles. *Instead of eating!*

I continue to replay all the mistakes I made this morning by only feeding the loudest screaming pain in my body. As I continue to sip my electrolytes in anger, I can't help but take every step with more gusto as I plant my foot exactly where my eyes carefully select.

I continue the climb to the top of the ridgeline. As I try and catch up on my hydration, sipping on some electrolytes, I leave a little of the moisture in my mouth to aid the absorption of a gel pouch. I reach into my shorts pocket to find one. I quickly look at the packet to ensure my eyes aren't off the path for too long. I look to see what flavour to expect, as some are a rude shock that a fragile mind needs to be prepared for. It's sour apple with caffeine. *Great. Not what I need right now.* I search the other pocket for a caffeine-free gel. I couldn't find one. *Just great, another thing, I've not even packed my pockets properly this morning. What else have I forgotten?* I search for the green khaki shirt. *I can't spot it.* How far behind am I slipping? *Will I make it to the checkpoint in time to continue through for the rest of the day?* For the first time this morning, I fathom the twenty-seven kilometres that follow checkpoint one. I haven't thought that far ahead. I realise now just how important it is to come back into focus. I move as fast as I can until I reach the top of this hill. I lean first on a method I've come to use occasionally when in a funk, one I learnt from the wisdom of Wayne Dyer's '101 Ways To Transform Your Life'. It's the simple method of recounting the word 'love' as often as possible. Repeating the word inside my head repeatedly catches me from overcalculating steps. As my foot hits an unsuspectingly loose rock, the moment of frustration is quickly diffused when I remember to recount the word love. It's a split second between wanting to somehow destroy the rock to having that thought melt when I'm meant to love. The replayed word gets me almost to the top of the ridgeline. As I feel the top getting closer, the repeating words method begins to fade in effectiveness.

The next thing I focus on is a method learnt from Hanny Allston, the runner who mapped the program I followed during training for these four days. Her invisible button method is a way of capturing just one moment on a run that feels good. A time at which you are perfectly fuelled, perfectly hydrated, your clothes sitting just right, your body feeling good, and the moment being totally blissful. If you squeeze your thumbs into your hands, like you're clicking an imaginary button, you revisit those conditions in the mind and feel the sensation across your body. The moment beneath my imaginary button is a run I enjoyed one day, along the beachfront path from Mermaid Beach to Miami Hill. It was about 10am, and the sun was shining across the ocean to show a glaring sparkle, the breeze was cool, and the path had died down of the morning walker traffic, having only a few people around. I'd had breakfast, a coffee and was perfectly hydrated, and the moment felt as though it was something that could only be enjoyed by the most privileged of people. Free, fit and grateful. As I continue to squeeze the imaginary buttons and visualise the flat path I've learnt every detail of over the last year of my life, I get incredibly close to the top of the ridgeline.

As I scramble toward the sky, rather than more rock, I watch runners coming from my left running toward my right. I begin to follow them, before I see a volunteer who directs me first to the left.

"That way, first love. It's worth it!" She joyfully directs, pointing at the other runners. I begrudgingly follow the path and run against the other runners, spotting the man in the khaki shirt. *I hope this little detour that I'm yet to do isn't long.* It looks like the ridgeline is coming to an end. Why are we running this way? I watch as a couple of woman thread themselves through a couple of trees, grinning from ear to ear, energised as they sing their goodbyes to whomever they're leaving behind. They look revived. As I get to the tree line, I slow down to weave myself through the trees. On the other side is one of the race volunteers with a clipboard, who searches his pages for my number.

"Enjoy the view!" He says, as he opens his arms, referencing all that's behind him.

It's almost as though the sound of his words brings into focus exactly what I'm looking at. A large chasm separates us from a razor-like sharp rock, that is striped with different shades of red, and as though its paper-thin and pierced through the earth, lodged like a glass shard.

I take quick and deep breaths as I attempt to catch my breath and breathe in the incredible view. I try to find a spot for my sore feet to stop solidly and firmly on the ground. I move and sway, looking for comfort, to no avail. I don't take my eyes from the view, stumbling as I try to find my feet. I'm interrupted from my daze.

"I can take a photo for you if you like?" The volunteer offers.

"Oh yeah, that'd be great," I reach for my phone.

He captures the photo, and I take my phone and glance at the time.

"I'd better get going if I'm going to make checkpoint one," I say.

"Have another minute, Karlee," the gentleman assures. "You'll make it."

"Will I?" I ask, genuinely concerned.

"Yeah, just stay where you are in the group and you'll be fine," he confirms.

I glance back out across the viewpoint. It's as though the view has become clearer with the relief seeping through my body. Feeling my toes relax ever so slightly in my shoes, I realise how clenched my feet have been all morning, as they attempted to keep my feet landing precisely, ensuring my ankles stay upright. I can feel the toenail beds on the outside of my left foot. As I inspect the lines in the razor-like rock ahead, I feel the pulse of my toes and know the toenails will soon lift away from the beds. I'm amazed I've not been able to feel those toes yet, as they lose their nails, after being masked by a louder pain.

It's as though the more I feel in my body, the more I can see of the view. I begin to worry about just how cold my joints are getting as they stand stationary. I decide it's time to leave, just as I hear the arrival of the runner behind me. I see it's a familiar face. Ben, who has run far too closely behind me for the last two days. As I spot him, I decide it's time I shuffle along, and quickly.

I move as quickly as I can across the top of the ridgeline, and while I no longer contend with the uphill climb, I now face the challenge of believing I should be able to move quicker, now that I'm on flat ground. Yet, the pace is almost the same, as it's a bigger struggle to pick any kind of path, or trail where feet have landed before me. Sure, I move quicker, but my eyes struggle to pick the best line of where to plant my feet. As a result, the terrain beneath my trail shoe moves and shifts, reminding my ankles of the day's prior torture on a loose pebbled descent. I continue to move as quickly as possible, my eyes not lifting from the ground beneath me.

Before long, my dazed concentration is interrupted by a voice behind me. Ben has caught up to me, and I'm immediately feeling defeated, and no longer silently in my pain cave. He announces his presence and asks once again if he can follow my pace and run behind me. For the third day in a row, the pleasantries overtake me.

"Sure!" I say politely, hiding the break in my voice as I battle with emotion.

It doesn't take long for Ben to realise I'm not up for chatting and need to focus on my footing. He stops talking and just quietly runs behind me. Part of me doesn't mind having him behind me; it urges me to move slightly faster and maintain some kind of rhythm.

I'm eagerly awaiting the ridge to take a downward turn, which would indicate I'm nearing checkpoint one, but the ridge just keeps on going. I check the time to see how long until the cutoff. 15 minutes. The urgency of time makes me naturally pick up the pace. As I speed up, I realise that it's not possible for me to pick safe lines while going so fast. I start to slow down again when I feel a sharp knock to my ankle.

"Oops, sorry!" I hear Ben shout from behind.

Turning my head slightly, I realise he's hit my ankle with his poles. It infuriates me, not just because of the pain and how sensitive my ankles are, but for the pure fact that he's using the poles on the flat ridge line. I try to let it go and continue moving.

The ridgeline takes a sudden turn, and I see the beginning of the descent down to checkpoint one. I'm relieved and begin the descent quickly, before I'm reminded that the downhills are my most painful times. Almost instantly, my thighs begin to tremble under the pressure of trying to hold myself upright and not take a tumble down the sharp red rocks. My pace slows. I focus intently on picking each step, feeling sharp pain each time my foot lands on the earth. As I take more careful steps, I'm snapped back to the moment once more with another hit on the ankles. Ben has pierced my ankle again with his pole. His silence and mine follow. I take a deep breath and swallow all the words that are about to blurt from my mouth. It reminds me of the last time I swallowed my words, just kilometres ago, as I climbed the shady side of this ridgeline, when I was recounting the word 'love.' I try hard to think of the word and recount it in this moment of frustration. But all I think of is how I don't love those stupid bloody poles.

The descent continues, and I feel the repetition and pain

clutching more and more tightly onto my lower limbs. Each step becomes increasingly careful. The descent now is not only reliant upon my legs, but my hands too, as they hold onto rocks and guide me carefully down the cliff face. I know I'm moving slower than most, but these descents are when the body feels at its weakness.

"Do you want my poles?" Ben pipes up from behind.

"No, thank you!" I reply bluntly, without needing a second to consider. "You can go ahead if you'd like," I offer in an attempt to get him out of my space.

"It's alright - we're nearly at checkpoint one," he says.

At the base of the cliff is a 4WD track that hugs the large rocks. As I cruise along the track, I begin to hear other voices, and I know we must be approaching checkpoint one. No sooner do I make out the voices than Ben finds a quick pace and speeds off ahead, as he has done for the past few days. It frustrates me. Because of all the time he's spent far too closely following behind me, he finds an impressive energy to put on show for the volunteers.

I reach the checkpoint right on the cut-off time and begin to unpack my vest in order to top up my electrolyte bottles and water bladder. This is the first and only checkpoint for the day, so it means we must carry a full load of water, which essentially isn't as much as I'd like to take out into the bush for a twenty-seven-kilometre stretch. But the harsh terrain does not allow for any checkpoint stations to be propped up throughout, so we must simply get as loaded as possible and then run our butts off right to the finish line.

I sip at water and chew on fruit cake with one hand, as I reapply antichafe cream beneath my bra line with the other. I consciously try not to drink too quickly to ensure I don't get a stitch. I see Ben has pulled off his shoes and socks, and I see a moment of opportunity to get on the path before he's ready and hopefully move off far enough ahead to be alone and free of any poles that could stab my ankles. I scan the bench where I've placed my vest to make sure I have all my belongings. I feel the chest tubes to make sure they're full, grab a handful of lolly snakes and bid the volunteer who's been assisting me farewell. Just like that, I'm off and alone on the track again.

As my shuffle gets quicker, I begin to find my familiar pace. It's a pace that feels manageable yet is moving as quickly as possible. As I settle into a rhythm in gently undulating hills, I begin to realise what I've just done. I've just made it through checkpoint one, and now, there's nothing between here and the finish line. I think back to this morning. *I genuinely feared making it this far!* I needed to reach checkpoint one quickly if I wanted to have the opportunity to finish the rest of the day and the entire four days.

20

I continue jogging as quickly as I can, taking the opportunity to run while the path underfoot is hazard-free. I move at a rapid pace to ensure I can be left alone on the track without Ben catching me. I watch as flashes of colour capture my eyes, and I slow my pace to see incredible colours beneath my feet. Due to some natural wonder, there are big changes in colour in the dirt beneath me. Big sections of sand-like colour, into red, and some parts even being purple. I marvel at the colours beneath my feet, slowing down slightly whenever I see two colours meet. As I slow down this time, I'm met with more colours than just the different clays. I spot some bright purple wildflowers. I pull out my phone to capture the colours, and as I take in the beauty, I realise that just for a moment, I hadn't thought about my feet or racing away from the closely following company. I have just been here with the colours of the outback and the wildflowers.

As I bask longer in the beauty that surrounds me, I feel the noise and tension from my brow begin to ease. I realise how far away from these red hills I've been for the morning. My mind hasn't been here at all. *I've been so occupied by the pain of the first few kilometres, then occupied by having someone far too close behind me, that I've forgotten to appreciate exactly what I'm doing! I'm on day 4 of running the Larapinta Trail. A wonder that only a few will ever get the chance to enjoy! I've trained hard for this, I paid to be here, and I'm not allowing myself to enjoy it.*

I look up to the hot sun sitting high above me, and I feel the muscles in my neck stretch. It reminds me just how little I've looked up over the past four days. I'd spent most of my time looking at my feet and carefully choosing my line of path to ensure I stayed upright. I feel sad at the realisation of how much beauty and views I've possibly missed by doing so. *I wanted to do this run for me. I wanted to enjoy being out here in the middle of the outback, taking in the incredible red ridgelines, yet I've watched my feet the whole time. I gifted myself this time, and I robbed myself of enjoying it too.* As I continue to shuffle along, a sudden urge to stop comes over my legs, and my feet stop instantly. I decide that rather than running as fast as I can in the parts that are easy underfoot and take less attention to choosing my steps, for the remainder of the day, I'm going to take in the views and try my best to enjoy myself. I'll look up, while my eyes don't need to carefully consider their steps. *I'll take in the sights while I'm here.*

I'm not sure if it's the fact that every step is taking me closer to the finish line, or if it's the appreciation of my surroundings, but the pain seems increasingly manageable. I have pain in most parts of my legs, but I know now they'll hold me until the end. After all, there's no other way to get out of here now, other than running or an emergency evacuation.

The sound of Ben's voice soon disturbs me from my peace. He immediately questions if I'm injured, due to the slower pace I'm taking on the flat sections.

"No, I'm just taking the chance to enjoy the view," I state calmly. "You're welcome to go right ahead," I urge.

"It's okay, I should enjoy it too," he realises.

As we continue to cruise along the undulating hills, with a solid and clear path underfoot, Ben circles back to the few things we'd bonded over when we first met on day two. One being that we were both from the Gold Coast, the other being that he knew Aiden, the man I'd once cared for. He mentions Aiden again today, just as I'm starting to wonder whether my toenails are still attached. I can't help but find it frustrating that in an endeavour I set out to do entirely alone, and for myself, I continued to be here, caring for others. I was showing a great deal of kindness toward Ben because we had a mutual connection, but the reality is, I didn't want to be the one pacing. I didn't want him following me and hitting my ankles with his walking poles. I owed him nothing. I'd paid good money and gone to great lengths to get here, with the strength and fitness to run for four days in this incredible landscape. As I continue to grapple with why I feel inclined to let Ben follow me, somehow feeling symbolic of caring too much for those that I've cared for in the past, I feel another clang of his walking pole pierce my ankle.

This time, the pole lodges itself into my shoe and pulls the pole from his grip. I stop to dislodge the pole from my shoe and return it to him with no words. He apologises sincerely. Of course, he's not meaning to hurt or disturb me, but I feel the last of my kindness for someone else, out here in the elements, leave me.

"Do you really need two poles on flat ground?" I ask, handing the pole back.

"No, not really. I've just been too lazy to fold them away into my pack," he declares, as he reaches for his backpack belt and begins unbuckling it from his back.

"Well, take your time. I'm going to find somewhere down there to wee." I point downhill to a little collection of shrubs.

"Then, how about you keep pushing ahead? I wouldn't mind being alone for the rest of the day," I say sternly as I head off track away from him.

"Yeah, okay. Are you sure you'll be alright?" He asks, as though he's had some kind of influence over my journey so far.

"Absolutely. I'm just fine," I say as I scramble off track towards some bushes.

As I find a quiet spot behind the shrubs, I take a deep breath to breathe in the wild overgrowth that lies beneath me while off track. I lied about needing a wee. *At no point over the last four days has this body had ample liquid in its system that needed releasing while on trail.* I needed to remove myself from him and find the courage to set a boundary between me, this massive adventure, and the need to be polite to a stranger who has now injured me three times. I peer from behind the shrubs and watch as Ben journeys off ahead. I wait to give him plenty of time to get out of sight, because the last thing I want is to still have him lingering in sight as I round the next corner or climb the next hill. I just want to be alone.

I continue putting one foot in front of the other, each step getting me closer to Ellery Gorge, the finish line of the entire four days, with a water hole for a swim. The track becomes increasingly defined the closer I get to the major attraction on the track. Before I know it, I'm keeping my eye out for small metal track markers to show me how many kilometres are left before I kick these trail shoes off and relieve my feet of the tight strapping tape.

I enjoy being alone in my own company for the last few kilometres, but I begin to feel sorry for my body that has longed for a good rest for some time now. I consider the fact that I've given myself this experience as a gift, but the toll currently feels far from any gift. The challenge and immense satisfaction that comes from conquering this physical endeavour, as well as the thirty days of running for mental health, have been unlike anything I've ever experienced in life before. There's a special connection that has been formed in the throes of both challenges. A special relationship between body and mind. An ability to communicate their intricate needs, sometimes not on the same page as one another. When my body screams for rest or repair, my mind can overcome it. The physical pain is rarely able to stop me from continuing to strive towards whatever challenge I've set for myself. I felt these last four days added another layer of grit to all I've done before. Not just the running day after day as #KDOGONTHEJOG, but the Karlee who battled many quiet and directionless months alone inside her own head. From not feeling anything to being out here able to push myself physically, I've had it all over the last four days, but it's been far from silent.

As I get closer to Ellery Gorge, I feel like I've never been closer to myself than right now. I've watched myself over the last 4 days hold myself and carry myself through all kinds of emotions. As uncomfortable as it was to draw a fierce boundary between my own peace and Ben's walking poles, it was a moment that needed to happen. A moment that reminded me of my own peace being just as important as kindness.

♥

I've really enjoyed the last seven months, especially the months following the Run Larapinta. I bought a van after returning home from Tasmania, and although I was still living in my Mermaid Beach unit, the van provided the private sanctuary I was longing for. I'd spend my Wednesday through to Sunday mornings caring for Harry, then I was free every day by midday. I still rose early to move my body at sunrise, but I hadn't run much since Larapinta. At most, I would jog two to three kilometres at the start of my morning just to get the blood pumping. From there, I'd begin to feel the strain on lower leg muscles, particularly the outer muscles that ran down my left side. The sensation was as though my legs needed warming up, so that's exactly what I'd do each morning at sunrise. I'd finish the morning with a coffee at my local café, then journey off to Harry and Catherine's house in Palm Beach. I'd been working on the launch of Seed A Smile in my days, and now with the van, that was very much like a portable office where I could park up at a nearby beach or property and dive into my creative zone.

I'd been open to meeting other men, and feeling confident in my own skin, I would spark up conversations at the pub or the coffee shop. However, since the advance of social media and online dating, many people struggle to talk to strangers at all now. Many of my advancements on good vibing blokes would simply result in them getting nervous and ignoring me or walking away. Then, if I had the patience to chat to someone online, things would be fine on a first date, but nothing worth singing from the rooftops about. My general disinterest would eventually become too evident. I haven't met anyone as familiar as Tim Bayer, the guy who went to Antarctica, stopped speaking to me, yet watches my life unfold on Instagram stories every day.

That is, until just now. Opening my phone to check my notifications before hitting the road, there's a message on Instagram from 'Timmyb313.' I can read what I think is most of the message from just the push notification on my locked screen. Part of me hopes there's nothing more to the message, as it's perfect as is. But the rest of me needs to immediately open to see what else he might have said.

'I've been thinking about you… a lot.' *The whole message. Nothing else.* I read it over and over again and feel more emotion every time I do. I've wondered for the last seven months if I've overdramatised the time we spent together in Tasmania. I was convinced that it would be one of those perfect examples of love never running on time. I thought it would be the case that I'd meet someone else, and so would Tim, and life would go on. But I always thought about the most familiar stranger I'd ever met. It had made me wonder more about other lives, and past lives, as I still couldn't explain the familiarity of Tim, nor how easy it was to be around him and explore Hobart together.

I think about all the things I'd like to say in response. Finally, I decide I need to keep it simple, too. I hesitate over the message. *Should I give it a couple of hours?* But I'm conscious of the time difference and whether he'll be online again today. I don't want to lose my window.

'Well, I've thought about you lots too,' I write in response. I watch as the grey 'delivered' signal beneath the message changes to 'seen.' I await his response, sitting in my van, with the keys in the ignition. I leave our direct message window and scroll through Instagram for a while, to stay online and await his response. Nothing ever follows.

21

A year on, I roll back into the driveway in Miami, where I've stationed Seed A Smile's workspace and my office. When Hannah and I wrapped up our lease at the start of the year, I wasn't prepared to renew anywhere. Rent prices had skyrocketed on the Gold Coast, and my van Stella already felt like home for most of the week. The only limitation was that I needed somewhere to store pots and fulfil orders for my small business. My mate, MD, who was always good company for a beer, offered to set up his garage space in his house in Miami. That was the final piece of the puzzle. I'd move full-time into my van.

Nothing about the decision scares me. I have become so good at living on my terms, even the usual hiccups of 'Goldy' life hardly fazed me. Not the traffic, the construction, the chaos. In my world, I'm running a business that spreads kindness and plants. I'm salty from ocean swims, and I've still got smoke in my hair from a recent campfire. Life's simple. It's intentional.

Van life is vibrant, never the same, and incredibly healthy. My fridge is tiny, wedged between the driver and passenger seat, so I shop smart and eat fresh. I buy from the farmers' market, that way the fruit and veggies stay fresher for longer, stowed in the shade under my bed. Everything has a place. Leaving one item out of order feels like chaos. So, I constantly reset and restore order in my little sanctuary.

The van was not designed for living in. It was built to be an occasional camper. It's very aesthetically pleasing. No sliding drawers or kitchen cupboards. Just a single wooden bed frame in the back that opens to a double (though that option rarely suits my fiercely independent life). Underneath the bed beside my fruit basket is a shallow tub of thoughtfully rolled clothes. My kitchen gear lives in a second tub with access from the back door. One fry pan, one saucepan, and all the washing-up bits. My folding table is easily reached, ready for dinner under the stars. And the only storage cupboard is behind the driver's seat. Well, it's magic! No shelves, just a wooden box with three doors. But I know exactly where everything goes. Where it lands once the van rattles on the road, I can open a door, reach in, and my hand will land on exactly what I was looking for.

But today, as I roll into the driveway at Miami, Stella feels more like a tin can than my home. I ache. My lower back screams from the five-hour drive. I haven't run in weeks, only managing short walks and stretches before settling in at my desk for the day. A celebrant course has swallowed my schedule. I jumped at the chance to become an authorised celebrant for a friend's wedding. In hindsight, I didn't give myself enough time to comfortably complete it. Each day starts at the beach, followed by coffee, before visiting Harry for my morning care shift, and then I finish at my desk until bedtime.

I'm the lightest I've ever been. Fittest too, in body and mind. This body has carried me through deserts, over mountains, and between cities. So why? Why now does it feel like it's breaking down?

I've just come back from another trip to Taree, where Tim lives. He returned from his trip to Antarctica in April. Truthfully, I thought I'd be the first person he'd want to see. But he took his sweet time re-entering the world. I almost gave up on him. When he eventually asked to catch up for a beer, I said yes. But only once it suited me. I'd made plans on the day he suggested, and for the first time, I wasn't holding my breath.

Our reunion felt just like the day we met in Hobart. Only his dreadlocks had grown a little longer. We watched the local VFL team play. Tim sat on the picnic blanket with me, a van beer in hand, and settled into my world. We caught up on one another's adventures. He withheld showing pictures of Antarctica or penguins, but he was quick to show me a picture of his new niece, Poppy. "The cutest baby ever," he said. I loved that.

That night, I asked him outright if we were just two friends catching up, or if there was something more. He said more. He felt it too; the sense that we'd shared a life before this one. But the next morning, he left early, and the goodbye was awkward. *Is this another goodbye where I'll be left wondering?*

"Come visit me in Taree," he said as he left.

But now, four months in, we're both making trips up and down the east coast of Australia. We've talked openly about the future and the effort required over the distance. He's made it clear. Taree is home. And I'm okay with that. Being near family, even if it's not my own, is what I want. I'm open to relocating in the new year. But every trip wears on me. It's as though my 1999 Mitsubishi Express van gets younger, while I get older. The tyres are fine. My body isn't.

Today, as I step out of Stella, I both long to stand and dread putting weight on my legs. My left leg is almost completely numb. My lower back tenses, and I'm unsure if I want to stretch it or curl up into a ball. I make it inside before I collapse on the green couch in my office garage. Tears stream down my face.

The pain is sharp and layered with exhaustion. I've held it together all weekend, in company. Smiling, standing, pretending I'm not hurting, and it's all caught up on me. *This shouldn't be happening. I'm the lightest I've ever been. The surgeon blamed the weight, and I believed him until now. I've done everything. Tried everything. Why is it unbearable now? Just as life is getting good.* I texted Tim to let him know I made it back safely. He instantly replies, 'Miss you already.' I cry harder.

With every tear, my mind conflicts. *I'm wildly in love. But I'm so embarrassed by this pain. Embarrassed by my legs. I'm sad for my body. I'm scared for the future. I feel like a burden. But I also feel completely loved.* It's all happening at once. Joy, shame, fear and love. Coexisting in my crumbling body. I don't want pain to define this chapter, but it is. It's as though I'm standing at the exit of a cave. The light ahead, I worked so hard for. But the cold shadows the path, keeping me there.

As I stare at the ceiling, I swallow deep breaths through the pain. I realise I'm most afraid of becoming a burden. That isn't who I am. *I'm the carer. I'm the giver. I'm the one who keeps it all together. I'm the one who makes it easier for everyone.* But now, I can't leave this chapter and start the next without help. I can't do it without being looked after. I hate that. It's not who I am. It's not who I've been.

22

I've been living in Taree with Tim, and his best mate's Sam and Jordan, for just under a month. Their house is brand new, full of sunlight and shared meals; a far cry from my little van. They live well together. They cook, eat and laugh together as a team. It's warm here. And for now, I'm job hunting, which is overwhelming.

Jordan is heavily pregnant, and today she's proposed we all take a trip to a beach I've yet to visit. A few minutes into the drive, my left hip begins to throb. The deep, dull, familiar ache that's moved from annoying to inhibiting. I wriggle in my seat, but the pain just shifts.

"How far's the drive to Saltwater?" I ask casually, as though I'm just curious to learn.

"It's about twenty minutes," Tim replies. "Is that alright?" He asks, turning to face me in the back.

"Yeah! Course! I was just wondering!" I assure him with a smile.

I feel every second of the twenty-minute drive that follows. By the time we drive around the parking area twice to decide on the best parking spot, I am almost on the verge of tears. I fear how I will be able to cover this pain when it comes time to get out of the car. As we park up, I try my best to get out of the car quickly. As my legs straighten out and I feel the earth beneath my feet, I search for any reason to stand still for a while. As I do, I spot the tube of sunscreen in our beach bag, and quickly begin to smear it over my face. As I rub in the sunscreen, I feel the tension across my face, attempting to relieve it as I rub in my sunscreen. Tim and Jordan chat while I continue rubbing in the sunscreen, waiting for my legs to find sensation.

"Ready, Sis?" Jordan asked, checking on me.

"You bet!" I say, in an eager facade. "Where are we heading exactly? Is it very far?" I question.

"Nah! Just down there," she references a small arch in the trees that peeks a glimpse of the water.

As we find a spot on the sand to lay out our towels and ditch our bags, I'm eager to get in the water. I'd never felt this degree of pain in the peak of summer, and it was a bizarre sensation to feel so stiff, almost cold in the bones, while my body was overheating. I'm excited to get in the water and float; that's always a good sensation. As I kick off my shoes and attempt to walk over the sand, I feel uneasy on my feet as the loose sand moulds beneath my feet. My ankles vividly think back to the loose rubble of Larapintas Day 3 descent, as I carefully move toward the water. Looking at Tim, I realise he's seen my struggle.

"It's a bit bloody hot!" I say, smiling.

"Well, it's lovely in here!" He yells from the water.

I tackle the few steps across the loose sand and try to keep my face as neutral as possible. As I do, I feel the familiar band-like sensation strap tightly across my forehead and jaw line, like what I felt living with Anna. As my feet enter the water, it provides a slight moment of cool relief, and I continue walking further in. I still strain to keep my footing beneath me, as the sand melts and moves out from under my feet. I move my way toward Tim, but as I do, I realise he's quite deep into the water. I make it to him, and we playfully embrace. I feel better just being in a moment together with Tim, just the two of us, alone and floating. No sooner do I relax do I realise how strong the current is. It's moved us a good few metres already, so we both stand up and begin to reposition ourselves. Tim stands quickly and takes about four big strides as the water laps around his thighs. As I stand up, I feel the sand move beneath my feet and instantly know these steps will challenge me. As I attempt the first step, always by leading with my right foot, all the sand moves away under my toes, and the current grabs at my knees. The pain is so much that I'm not even sure which part of my left leg is screaming the loudest; it's just as though there's a chorus line of pain, from the centre point of my arse cheek to the outer skin on my thigh, to a searing pain in my groin. I can't hold in the noise that escapes me as I attempt the big necessary strides against the current.

"You right?" Tim asks as he holds out his arms for an embrace.
"Yeah, just a bit sore," I admit.
"Hips?" He wonders aloud. I have told him to a degree about the pain I've been experiencing.
"Yeah, the bloody hip," I say in defeat as Tim takes hold of me in the water with a loving smile.
"These hips don't lie!" He jokes, bringing a smile to my face.

"Shakira, Shakira!" He sings.

We take in the surroundings for a little while, looking at fish and obscure shaped trees on the other side of the inlet. And as we do, the current continues to demand my legs to hold me strong. I decided to get out of the water rather prematurely. I don't attempt to move against the current back to where we entered; instead, I just walk directly up the sand and slowly make my way back once out of the current's grip. Keeping just enough water over my feet, to hopefully explain my carefully placed footsteps. I make it back to the towel and lie down, but not before moving several times to try to find a comfortable spot to rest. I even attempt to dig a little sand out from under my towel to adjust the angle of my glutes, inspired by the large hole Jordan has dug for her big, beautiful belly to sit in, which allows her to lie face down without squishing her baby.

Tim eventually makes it back out of the water and sits next to me on the sand. As he returns, I attempt to make just one last shift for a while to appease my agitated legs and not draw any attention to my discomfort. Tim brushes off his towel and immediately relaxes alongside me. I somehow share a piece of that relief, as I admire the muscles in his body relaxing, and listen to him sigh. Both Tim and Jordan lay peacefully still, basking in the February sunshine. I grapple with my irritated legs to remain still, internally bargaining with myself on why I should remain still. But there's a power in restless legs that is beyond anything the mind can control, and I've learnt in the recent weeks sleeping next to Tim that the more you attempt to fight them, the larger the jolts will be. In response to my head trying to remain still and relaxed on the beach like Tim and Jordan, my legs go out in rebellion, making a few large jolts across the sand. As they do, I immediately sit upright on the towel to stop them.

"What's up, Karls?" Jordan asks, knowing something isn't right.

"Ah, it's all good. It's just my stupid hip."

"I didn't know it was this bad. I've been watching you. You've not been able to stop moving your legs," she points out sternly.

"Yeah, I don't know, it's been really bad since I got here," I try. Finally, I let go.

"I don't think the drive helped, and then a new bed maybe," I explain.

"Does it ever stop hurting?" She wonders, genuinely concerned.

As I listen to her question, a wave of possible answers that undersell my pain comes to the forefront of my mind, as they've always done when discussing my discomfort. But, as I stumble on my words, I figure the truth may explain my lack of action in finding jobs or being a bubbly person to live with.

"No, not really," I admit, as my voice begins to break. At this point, Tim sits up alongside me to get a better look at my face.

"Never?!" Jordan asks, shocked. As she does, I can't help but let a few tears escape.

"It's pretty shit," I let out. Tim moves closer and pulls me to look at his face.

"Are you crying?" He tenderly teases, as he has said countless times over the past six months. During our time together so far, I have let go of many overwhelmed tears. Whether it be our goodbyes, our reunions, sharing news of my nephew's arrival, or recounting the day I told Harry that I'd no longer be able to care for him, Tim had seen a lot of tears. But these tears were different.

"Well, what are you going to do about it?" Jordan demands.

"I don't know." I declare. The entire narrative of how I've quietly managed the pain for years lies ready to flood out.

"I just can't do all the things that used to make me feel good anymore," I continue. "I've managed the pain just fine for years. But now, I'm at a point where I can't go a day without taking strong painkillers, and I hate that."

I let go quickly, and with more tears.

"It's like they don't even work! They just make it harder to hear the pain. I used to know exactly which muscle hurt and how to relieve it. I used to know if I was sore, just to take it easy. But now it's just constant."

"Aw, darling. That's horrible. I had no idea it was that bad," Jordan comforts. "But, what now? What's your next step?"

"Ah, I just need to focus on getting a job first," I begin. "I need to get money coming in so I can find a new doctor and maybe get some scans. I might need to find an osteopath or physio for some temporary relief. I just know it'll all add up really quickly."

"Babe. Just do it. I can pay for it all," Tim quickly urges. This makes me crumble even more in emotion, for I know he genuinely just wants me to be out of pain.

"Yeah, I know," I quietly confirm. "It's just that I know what the fix will ultimately be."

"What? A new hip?" Tim quickly fills in.

"Yeah, a new hip," I confirm.

"Well, that's alright, isn't it?" Jordan wonders.

"Yeah, it's fine," I confirm.

"It's just that it all is so far away. It's going to be months and months of this." I let out more tears as Tim holds onto me tighter.

"My head is just a mess. I'm so happy, but…" I look to Tim, worried he'll be scared of what follows next.

"…But I'm also not at the same time. I can't afford to get any worse. It just makes me so sad. I don't feel like half the person I really am. And I have no idea why any of you, or your friends, would be interested in meeting this Karlee," I reveal to Tim.

"Babe, that's silly. I love you. And that's all that matters." He gives me a little shake in his embrace. "I don't want you living in pain, though. No one does."

"And... Everyone who meets you always talks about how much they love you. So, you need to stop being worried about that," Jordan demands, as she carefully moves her pregnant body to come closer to me.

They both let me cry as they sit on either side of me on the sand. And again, I'm caught in between feeling immense happiness for their genuine support and the overwhelming weight of my pain.

♥

Jordan and Sam welcome their baby boy on the exact night Tim and I move out. We settle into the spare room of his cousin Rohan's house in Wingham, just out of Taree. Rohan and his wife, Sarah, are renovating their charming century-old home, and they've kindly opened it to us for a couple of months before we move into a unit in town.

Rohan and Sarah are delightful homebodies. He loves DIY projects, while Sarah tends to her native flower garden after work. They're both physios at the Mayo private hospital, and living with them is very calming. There's no television, just a record player.

During the days I'm home alone, working remotely in my new full-time role at Ovatu.

Ovatu is a global booking system run by a lovely couple in Berry, NSW. They received thousands of applications for the job, and thankfully, my tactful, bright orange resume stood out. I had no customer support background, but they saw the human beyond that. After one Zoom interview, they offered me a hybrid role supporting both our customers and the head of operations. It's flexible, varied, and fun. I work from home, in whatever clothes my aching hip needs. Often a robe, rarely pants.

The new job brought more than an income. It gave me the freedom to start sorting out my health. It took weeks to find a GP who would take a new patient and really listen. I took a growing list of concerns: constant left hip pain, a resulting limp that's messing with my feet, loss of menstrual cycle, and a mental load that's getting heavier. The flexible job allowed me to juggle appointments, and I was upfront with my manager on that front. *But I still feel guilty. I've just started, and I'm asking for so much.*

Tim supports me wholeheartedly, and so do Rohan and Sarah. There's no conversation off limits around the dinner table. And one night, they gently suggest I reconsider the specialist I'm about to see. He isn't one they recommend. They know surgeons by their results. With their encouragement, I get into someone better and sooner.

Rohan also offered to assess my mobility one night if I was open to it. I am. So tonight, Tim's out with his mates having some beers, and Rohan has made some time for me. We've just finished

THE ART OF ~~LIVING~~ GIVING | 249

moving through the house using furniture as makeshift physio equipment. He demonstrates, and I follow. He watches closely to see how far I move, how long I hold and how quickly I wince.

"You should not be forcing yourself through any kind of exercise for the sake of trying to help your mobility," he softly explains. "I mean to say that anything you do with resistance is doing more harm than good at this point in time, yeah?" He wonders if I understand where he's coming from.

"Pretty much everything I do is done in resistance at the moment," I say only half jokingly.

"Exactly. I know that. I could see that," He agrees seriously. "There were certain movements that I began to show you that hurt you before you even tried. I watched your face grimace and hurt before you even moved into position. That's not helpful," he begins.

Rohan continues to explain in his well-educated tongue about many of the concepts I've been reading about in my attempts to study and learn about chronic pain. I was adamant that half of the pain was in my head, and it's like I begin to daze over the words that spill from his mouth, and instead, begin to feel incredibly validated. *He sees me. Quite the opposite of that surgeon years ago!*

He hands me notes scribbled on a used envelope. With terms like 'swimming' circled to highlight their kindness on my body, and a list of possible treatments that would assist the overall outcome for my health and happiness. What's not written or encompassed on the page is the fact that I feel entirely heard.

I don't feel an ounce of judgment for not moving as much as I have in the past, or for not weighing as little as I did when I was able to run and move freely. I didn't need to explain in its entirety the mental struggles it took to move or what the impacts of that meant. The page of notes also didn't explain just how freeing it was to speak up and be heard. Just as Tim and Jordan had listened on the beach that day, Rohan did the same and brought his expertise with it. What Rohan gave me tonight isn't just advice; it was some kind of release.

♥

It's been several months since I began searching for remedies. Scans, referrals, waiting rooms, heat packs, massage and second opinions. And now, it's just one week out from my hip surgery. A total hip replacement.

As I wake up on the top bunk of the small cabin full of women, I'm unsure what part of me hurts the most. Instantly feeling in need of fresh air, I quietly climb down the bunk bed ladder, attempting not to wake the inevitably hungover heads of Mal's mum and aunties who are sleeping below. I opted to stay in the cabin out the back of the big house we had rented for Mallory's hen's party in Lakes Entrance. Knowing I'd be off my anti-inflammatories in the lead up to the surgery, I pre-empted my need for space from the main party goers.

I hobble outside into the cool Victorian morning air and take a seat in the communal barbecue area that sits between both dwellings on the block. My head is clouded and heavy, with a cracking yet manageable headache. Without any serious maths, I know it's not only due to the alcohol I consumed last night, the uncommon amounts of sugar it was mixed with. We had a topless bartender hired to mix our drinks all night, and the drinks were delicious, but also incredibly necessary to handle the awkwardness of the man's presence. He was the only awkward part of the night.

I had been struggling with social settings ever since moving to Taree. Hindered with hip pain and having no way to clear my head without running, I felt anxious at the best of times. But being so wildly in love with Tim, I wanted nothing more than to be a lovely girlfriend, one who was worth showing off to all his friends and family. Yet the pain had impacted so much of my life that I'd be in a state of anxiety before I'd even reached the car. In fact, some of the worst moments were just getting into the car after having got dressed, in a body that had grown thicker with less movement. I didn't want any garment of clothing latching around my hips or legs, so I'd often reach for dresses that had wide waistlines, and come time to check my reflection, I'd just see someone who looked huge, with no waistline.

Often, the last step to leaving the house was putting on socks and shoes, both tasks that had become nearly impossible for me. Well, they were possible, but it wasn't without holding my breath and grimacing my face. By the time I'd meet Tim, who was ready and waiting, I'd feel pained, stressed and have my light face of makeup already running down my face (before even stepping foot outside the house!)

The thought of this hen's weekend had scared me. I only knew the hen, and had committed to spending a weekend with her and all her friends, who knew each other, with nothing in my system to help with the pain. To my surprise, I was quite relaxed and really enjoyed myself the first night. I blended into Mal's group of friends very quickly, and it was actually quite relieving to relax in a social situation, not having the self-imposed pressure of needing to be Tim's incredible girlfriend.

As I sit outside, trying to breathe in deeply, I quickly identify the familiar struggle of each breath becoming increasingly difficult. The more I try to focus on my breath, the more impossible it becomes. I know I need to quickly take my mind elsewhere and not think about my breathing. The psychologist I have been seeing in Taree has challenged me to count backwards from one hundred in multiples of seven when I become too aware of my breath. That and to lie down, remaining completely still.

Well, I'm not lying on the cold ground here! But I am prepared to do the counting thing. My mind continues to dart back to the tight breaths in my chest, and I get the urge to call Tim. He answers promptly, and his calming voice immediately makes me cry.

"Hello buddy," he says, in our usual greeting.

"Hey buddy," I respond in a defeated tone.

"Aww, babe. What's going on?" He quickly identifies that I'm crying.

"I'm just getting a bit worked up and need to be distracted," I explain quickly.

"You're safe though, yeah?" He asks quickly.

"Yeah, I'm safe. I'm just getting a bit stressed and needed… I don't know. I just…" before I can find the right explanation, Tim understands the assignment.

"Aw, well, that's alright. Dottie and I are here. She's being a laydown girl on mum's side of the bed. Aren't you Dottie?"

He starts talking to our beautiful dog, and it does make me feel a little better. Tim continues to hold the conversation and tell me about his day and what he and Dottie got up to the night before. Eventually, he hears my demeanour change throughout the call and can eventually start questioning me a little more about the night. I manage to explain to him that I'm having a really good time, but I've woken up in a pain-induced panic. He helps me talk through my next moves and ends the conversation by helping me focus on achieving a couple of tasks: having a shower and finding some coffee.

I attempt the coffee task first and wander through to the main house. The household of party goers is all sound asleep, so I'm sure to quietly file through the drawers and cupboards. It becomes a frantic search as the coffee potentially gets closer. Just like the moment your full bladder has made it to the bathroom, yet you can't take your pants off quick enough. I boil the kettle and find a mug, yet I fail to find any coffee. I curse the accommodation. *What kind of rental is this? Not even a stick of International Roast!*

I make my way back outside to the seat I was sitting in before. With a sense of defeat, my breathing becomes difficult again. I spend a good ten minutes trying to distract myself from focusing too intently on my breath. I quickly get a wave of feeling that tells me I need help, more so, I just need the presence of other people to keep me grounded. I make my way quietly inside the cabin, and I'm unsure of how I'm meant to tackle my next steps. I'm going to be waking Mal's mum, Kim, and time feels like it's been rewound. I feel like I'm ten years old, struggling to handle a sleepover. The nerves and emotions feel just as huge as being ten and asking for help from someone else's mum when all you want is your own.

Thankfully, as I make it into the bedroom, she is already awake and chatting to her sister in-law. Kim takes one look at me and knows something's not right. I watch her immediately sit upright in bed.

"What's wrong, darling?" She says tenderly.

"I'm just going into panic. I just need some help," I explain as bluntly as possible, refraining from getting emotional or beginning to cry. Somehow, she instinctively knows not to hug me and just comes to direct me firmly by the shoulders to the nearby couch. As she sits next to me on the couch, she doesn't let go of her firm hold on my leg, and I'm glad I asked for help. She sits quietly with me for a little while before she searches my face for permission to talk. Somehow, I express that I'm okay to talk.

"Have you had this happen before?" She tenderly asks.

"Yeah," I assure. "It's happened before. I will be alright," I say slowly, and quite disconnected as I fight the breath and words within my mouth. Almost as soon as I speak, a wave of sickness climbs its way up my body. I quickly get up to head for the bathroom, but as I reach the toilet, the feeling subsides. I feel like a goof now, just hunched over the toilet, with no more nausea. As I look up, I see Tanya at the door, a good friend of the hen and her family. Tanya has an angelic presence, as she instinctively knows that now is the time I need a big bear hug, as I hover in defeat by the toilet bowl.

"Have you had anything to eat or drink? Could that be worth a try?" She suggests.

"I did go in search of a coffee, but there's nothing in this entire place," I share in disgust.

"What?" She shares my shock. "What kind of accommodation

THE ART OF ~~LIVING~~ GIVING | 255

doesn't have coffee?" She shares. I'm instantly comforted, knowing I'm not the only one being dramatic.

I don't move far from the couch for the rest of the morning. People come and go, offering help, fruit, and tea. I grapple with how long I sit there in defeat of my own body and breath. I struggle to know what I need, but I know there are plenty of people here to help me find it.

I explain that I have a script for Valium that I've turned to in these states in the past, but I stupidly left it at home. I didn't take the same handbag on my trip to Victoria. It isn't long after I'd mention it that the beautiful bride-to-be arrived bearing a Valium.

When she enters the room, I cry, feeling sad that one of her partygoers is feeling so awful.

"I don't want you to think I'm not enjoying myself or wanting to leave! It's all just coming from the pain," I explain weakly.

She is totally understanding and even shares some of the pain quite literally. Her thumb and hand have swollen up after she bent them backwards, protecting herself from the ground under the load of the topless waiter, who, although we genuinely hired him to just make us drinks without a shirt on, took it upon himself to perform and inadvertently injured the bride. Recounting the moment together was a lovely and welcome momentary distraction.

I'm overly cautious about taking the Valium and want to be sure it doesn't jeopardise my surgery. I attempt to call any and every contact I think can give me an answer. My surgeon's admin team, my GP, and the hospital, yet no one can say conclusively. Adding to the stress, I end up listening to the quiet confidence of the collective ladies and just take the pill. I wait for the valium to kick in and do its thing, and it eventually settles in enough for me to catch my breath and start thinking logically about what I want to do for the rest of the day. The hen's party was planned with a sip and paint later that afternoon, before a glitter-themed night back at the house. I'd been genuinely looking forward to the day and was so excited over the glitter suit I bought in the lead-up, but the thought of waking up again in the same state tomorrow fills me with dread. Instead, I decide to call my parents, who are a four-and-a-half-hour drive away, to come pick me up.

I feel small once again as I dial Mum's number to explain. *What am I going to say?* I'd always tried to limit sharing my true struggle with my mum, for I never wanted to add to her worry. She was good at it. Her phone rings out, so I try my dad. Neither phone answers, which is out of character. The next person I call is my brother Billy.

"Karlee Warlee!" He quickly and joyfully answers, and I feel an immediate sense of relief.

"G'day Bill", I answer.

"How's the party?" Bill wonders, and I immediately know I need to cut to the chase.

"Party is good. But I'm just not coping. I've been having a panic attack for nearly four hours, and I just think I need to go. I can't get a hold of mum and dad," I quickly explain.

"Oh, Karlee! That's alright. We'll sort it out. Someone will come and get you, and you can just come home to Woodleigh. Mum and Dad are in at the accountants in Korumburra. I'll get in touch with them or make sure they get back to you as soon as they're done. It'll all be alright, yeah?" He comforts.

"Yeah, thanks, Bill!" We end the call without any of our usual jokes.

I spoke to Mum and Dad not long after the call with Billy, and Mum expressed that she didn't know how I'd handle the discomfort she'd seen me in before I left. *She wasn't surprised to get the call.* To help get me home sooner, I looked up how to get out of Lakes Entrance and at least en route in the direction of home, so it won't be such a long journey for everyone. There's a local bus I can catch that will take me to a train station. I can then travel in the direction of home, and let Mum and Dad know which station I jump off at and meet them at.

I pack and bid farewell to all the girls at the hen's party, except for the hen, who has gone out to get her suspected broken thumb put in a plaster cast. As I am preparing to leave for the bus, Tanya intercepts me and insists she drive me to the train station, so I don't need to catch the bus. A wave of relief rolls over me as I jump into her car. I am no longer in panic as such, but my full body is in immense pain. *It feels like I've just run a marathon at altitude with a dodgy hip!* Tanya attempts to keep the conversation going and isn't offended when I can't answer some of her questions.

I had taken a few calls from Tim throughout the morning, and he was trying his best to stay in the loop while being a state away. As I took this call in the car, I chatted to him as though no one else could hear the call. Knowing full well Tanya was right next to me, yet I'd gathered she was able to relate to me on many levels, even though we'd never met until last night. I spoke to Tim and explained what I was feeling. The sadness from leaving the party and feeling as though I hadn't celebrated my special friend. I explained what was going on in my body. The feeling of total exhaustion. I explained that Tanya was dropping me off at the train station, and I'd ride that for a few stops before meeting Mum and Dad. Tim listens and verbally hushes the overwhelming thoughts and guilt I have about leaving the party. His words perfectly address some of the concerns I poorly explained.

As I hang up the phone, I realise Tanya is crying, and I don't understand why.

"It's just so lovely to listen to you communicate. It's so special to witness two people navigating big emotions together," she sniffs.

I was thankful for Tim's help, but I didn't see it as anything out of the ordinary; but I suppose it is. As Tanya wipes her tears, she explains that she is just going to keep driving and take me wherever we'll meet my parents. I am overwhelmed with her kindness, having already been travelling for an hour and keeping her from the party. No sooner do I thank her, I feel my body relax, knowing that it doesn't need to compose itself for public transport. Soon after I felt my muscles relax, I asked Tanya to pull over the car. I just get the door open before I am sick all over the side of the road. *Why did that feel so good? Purging. Letting go. Letting kindness in.*

Having relaxed even further on the drive to meet my parents, I am ready to thank Tanya and greet my parents. I knew they'd let me do whatever I needed. As soon as I get in the car, I just sit and cry, trying to shut my eyes for some sleep. When I wake, my body immediately feels better, and I open my eyes to take in my surroundings.

"Ahh gosh!" I cry, waking from my sleep. "That's all I bloody needed. A stupid little nap," I declare in relief. My parents both laugh in shared relief.

"Ah, who would have thought, a stupid little nap was all you need!" Dad jokes.

My parents and I barely spoke a word of the panicked state I'd been in the whole drive home, but there was an unspoken feeling that we were all just glad to be going home.

The silence spoke louder than any conversation about my struggles. I had tried so hard to protect them from my suffering, trying to keep my dark cave hidden. I just had no idea it would feel so nice letting their light in.

23

The last thing Tim brings, or rather beckons over to me on the couch, is Dot, our loveable and lick-loving koolie cross kelpie dog. Dot's two very pointy ears drop down and slick back toward her slender waistline whenever she's in love mode. This means there's only about one stride and bound between her and her launching toward me in affection. As soon as Tim suggests, 'Come see mummy!' her ears instantly stick back as she changes gears for launch. Tim and my body immediately tense up as he moves as much of his body in front of mine. All I can do is cover my four-day-old surgery wound with my arms. Both bracing for contact, she drops her pace as she nears me, and thankfully, just climbs up my chest with her two front paws until she can reach my face for a lick.

Tim and I both relax, and he directs Dot up onto the couch over on his side, although there's room at my feet, which is actually

THE ART OF ~~LIVING~~ GIVING | 261

her spot on the couch. We try to keep her away from my freshly operated leg. I watch Dot's squirming puppy body eventually settle on the couch, and as she does, I feel my entire presence change. I'm in a state of peace here on this couch with my human and dog. It's unlike anything I've ever witnessed or felt before.

Tim's cuddled up nice and close, resting his head on the right side of my body. I become aware of his touch as I feel the weight of him on my body, and I compare that to the absence of pain in my left side. I don't think I've ever not felt my left hip, that is, until four days ago when I woke up from a total hip replacement at Mayo Private Hospital in Taree. It was the same sensation then, just far more sleepy. I woke up feeling nothing in my left hip joint. No conscious awareness that it was there, and up until now, it just never quite felt right at any moment in my day. I could feel the wound, and I can still feel that now, but that's a pain you'd expect to feel exactly how it does: tender, raw and pulsating with the throb of healing blood. But right here, as I lie on the couch with my legs up and Tim and Dot alongside me, I'm overwhelmed with happiness. The lightness in my physical body, even bearing a grand twenty-three centimetre-long fresh wound, is the most freeing feeling.

In the lead-up to the surgery, I'd wondered whether or not I was making the right decision, as I evaluated any possible complications. More so, my head had become so noisy that I'd actually wondered if I was in any physical pain anymore, or whether it was just my head. But today, this sensation, which is an absence of feeling, has given me all the validation I needed. *I lived in pain. Heavy, clutching, hindering and constant pain for years. A pain that existed in my life alongside everything I did, from getting comfortable in bed to sleep at night, to being an employee, to being a carer for someone else.*

"I'm so happy you're home," Tim interrupts my thoughts.

"Aww, so am I," I say with eyes that feel as though they're wider and no longer weighted by the furrow of my brow.

♥

In a scarily dazed state, I manage to pay attention to the words my mum says to Tim just as she's walking out the door. My eyes are struggling to stay open.

"You just come and wake me if she gets any worse," she softly yet sternly tells him, leaning in closer as she finishes. "We will just take her straight back to the hospital."

I'm immediately thankful she's said that, as I had battled with the same evaluation for the last hour, sitting in a sturdy outdoor chair in our loungeroom to aid my newly operated hip. It was not even a week old yet.

My mum had not offered, instead asking about her wellbeing, if she could come and help Tim and me after my surgery. This allowed Tim to continue working, and Mum to know firsthand that I was well and recovering just fine. When Dad and Mum drove in on Sunday afternoon, I was standing and walking around our front yard, barely relying on crutches. They couldn't believe how well I looked, and while Dad had endeavoured to drop Mum and continue north to their holiday house in Hervey Bay, I seemed so well that they thought Tim and I may not need the help.

However, Sunday night at the dinner table together, I quickly started going downhill with energy. By Monday afternoon, I was in hot and cold feverish sweats, battling flu-like symptoms. Physically, I was feeling so well on Sunday that I was thrilled to have three weeks off work with time to myself and my new, light leg. This was due to be my longest ever stint without needing to work, and on Sunday afternoon, I felt as though I was almost at the start of a holiday.

That feeling has long gone now, as I battle somewhere between a state of overheating, sleeping, and confusion. I'm scared and feel like my entire body has been shivering on the couch over the past four hours. I called my surgeon's team to explain my symptoms.

I thought I may have an infection, and was concerned for the implications that might have on a fresh wound. After asking how my wound looked and whether it was weeping at all, they weren't concerned that this had anything to do with my leg at all.

"You've probably just picked up a bug in the hospital," the team member had said on the phone.

As I watch Mum now walking out of the door, I watch Tim's demeanour soften as he's left in the house with just me and Dot. It's late, and Mum has already done all the dishes, so I anticipate Tim suggesting that we go to bed.

"Aww, babe." He comes in close. "Is there anything I can do?" He asks as though he's in pain watching me suffer.

"I don't know," I start to cry, now it's just us.

"Do you want a foot bath?" He asks eagerly. "A fruit cup?" he continues, listing all the little things that always make me feel better.

"I just want a hug," I sob in defeat.

"Aww. I can give my girl a hug," he says as he crouches carefully and awkwardly over my weak and injured body. "I can give my girl a hug whenever she wants it."

His words land deeper than I expected. I've asked for hugs before. From friends, from life, and I've been turned away. But now I really do feel I will be held whenever I need it. Tim will hug me whenever I need it. I relax into the hug and his care.

"Are you ready to get into bed?" He asks, watching my dread at the thought of standing up. "The sooner you do it, the sooner you can go to sleep," he coaxes.

Tim knows I need the encouragement, so he starts by reaching for my right sandal. He threads the one shoe onto my foot. It levels me out a little. The new hip has left me with a much longer leg on the left. One day I'll get the other done when I must. But not yet.

Tim stands close, holding both the chair firm and my arm, as I climb to my feet. The hip is working; it's strong. The height discrepancy is a massive adjustment. But it's the flu that has knocked all the strength from my arms, and it takes every ounce of energy to get out of the chair. I break my dazed state and stare directly at Tim. His eyes are so focused and attuned to every move I make, as though I'm fragile and precious. And for the first time, I believe I am.

♥

While it's only been eight months since my hip replacement,

I move peacefully in the cramped kitchen of our unit. As I dance between washing the dishes and stirring the frying vegetables, I hear the jingling of Dot's collar nearing, followed by the quiet shuffling of Tim's hardworking feet.

"Mmmm smells so shit!" Tim sarcastically jokes as he nears me for an embrace.

"Yeah, think I might just throw it in the bin, hey?" I joke in return, as I dry my hands, ready for his hug.

"I'm sorry. I'm not helping. Just sitting out in the lounge like a slob," Tim says, gently peeling himself out of the embrace to meet my eyes. I catch myself thinking of how I would have been frustrated by that in the past. Not only because I was standing in the kitchen on pained legs while others rested, but also if spoken to by ex-partners, I would have felt the remark was said to be polite. But Tim says what he means and means what he says. I feel for him, as I know he genuinely is sorry he's not helping.

"Babe, it's fine. You've been on your feet all day, and there's not much room in here for you to help," I assure him, reaching to stir the vegetables.

"Well, it won't be long until we're in our new home, and I'll be able to talk to you in the kitchen as you make my dinner, without leaving the couch!" Tim teases.

"That's right! Moral support!" I joke in return as Tim picks up the wooden spoon to stir the vegetables.

"I'm a bit of a tired boy," Tim says as he watches the moving vegetables, dazed.

"Yeah, same. We don't have to go to the gym every morning. It is a lot, but I would at least still like to rise that early to spend time writing my book," I say, continuing by washing the dishes.

"Maybe we don't go on Wednesday mornings. That can be

our little midweek rest day," Tim bargains, as he puts down the wooden spoon and meets my eyes. "Then you can spend more time writing on Wednesdays."

"Yeah, cool, that sounds good. Going to the gym four mornings a week is still great," I conclude.

"So, am I in this book?" Tim puzzles for the first time since learning I was writing a memoir.

"Yes babe," I instantly reply as though that would have been obvious.

"Aww… cool. Why and what are you writing about me then?" He asks worriedly.

"Babe, you definitely make it into the book. You may not feature as much as others, but you're kind of my happy ending, so of course you make it into the book," I explain matter-of-factly.

"Aw… really?" Tim asks, almost shocked.

"Yeah. Because of you, and moving here to live with you, meant I stopped having to hold everything together alone." As my eyes begin to get wet, I dry my hands again to reach for Tim. "You've made me feel like I have a story worth listening to, because you make me feel heard. You've listened to me." I manage to find my words through a trembling voice.

I peel myself slightly from the embrace to try and meet Tim's glance above me. As I find his welling eyes, he immediately draws me back into the hug.

"I've always been the one to fix, or listen, or fund. Just generally, I've always been the one to keep everything together. It was time for me to learn to be cared for. I really needed to be cared for."

I feel Tim grasp me tighter as we both take a synchronised breath through teary noses. "I think I kind of wrote this book for you, or at least because of you. See, I thought I was writing a book about giving. But really, I think I was writing my way toward receiving."

Under the weight of my ear, I hear Tim take some sharp, deep breaths into his chest, and I know exactly what he's saying in his silence. I know I've shown my gratitude for his care, and the hug between us holds more than just love. It's a hug that thanks one another for what we've been through together, but it also holds everything we've done for others in the past. As we both begin to exhale our next breath, our bodies simultaneously peel apart. The smile we meet each other with is lighter, as though a lot more than just our bodies were let go of there and then on that evening in the kitchen. There is so much that no longer needs to be carried.

24

It's another April morning, a year later. I hold our daughter Billie tightly to my chest as she suckles in for her morning feed. Dot sits with us on the bed, and us three of us have all been freshly smothered with kisses before Tim left for work.

I stare into Billie's alert blue eyes and soak in her spritely and cheeky energy that feels more and more exciting with every day she wakes. Nearing six weeks old, her smile is held reserved behind little coy smirks, yet I know she's a very happy baby, and the early mornings are my most favourite hours of the day with her.

My phone vibrates and I expect it to be a message from Mum in response to her firmly requested daily photo of Billie, but to my shock, I see the name Holly come across the screen. Considering it's been years between any polite interactions on socials and almost ten years since she was too busy to hug me on her trip to

Perth, my immediate thought is that she's sent a message to me by mistake.

Nervously, I open the message to see a long scroll of text. My heart sinks as I instinctively scan the message in search of its tone. My eyes find the words 'Billie,' then see the word 'support,' then the familiar 'xxx' to finish. I breathe relief as I begin again from the top to take in her words.

It's a kind and heartfelt message. She's a mother now to a young boy, and she has written to extend her best wishes. Like so many other young mothers around me, she was extending an encouragement to speak to her or anyone else if I was ever struggling. The words are raw, thoughtful, tender, and I can hear they're written from a place of struggle and hard-earned understanding.

I read the message repeatedly. Part of me is warmed and relieved by the message, but part of me also aches. Because I don't need support right now, I needed it back then, when I was twenty and needed a hug. Yet now, there's been an outpouring of support. Messages from all kinds of acquaintances near and far, all echoing a common theme of taking care of the mother. Ensuring she's eaten, showered, slept, and heard. It's beautiful, but it's baffling.

Because all of this care, the attention to my wellbeing, the frozen meals, the cards, the shoulder to cry on, the messages of reassurance, is what I needed years ago as a young carer. Back then, there was no tribe, no one shining the torch on the unsteady path. There was no one telling me that to care for someone else, I couldn't disappear myself.

Motherhood handed me the blueprint of care that I'd never been given before. It has given me what caregiving never did. A community, permission to rest and a wider understanding that my wellbeing is just as important. There's a real irony about it. How this chapter of life, that many find exhausting and overwhelming, to me, felt like a warm and healing hug.

I can't help but wonder where all this support was when I needed it. Even just the texts. They may not be able to physically carry a load or hug a crumbling girl struggling to make her cup of tea, but they can make a few minutes brighter; they can shine a light in a dark, mouldy apartment.

The truth is, our society isn't built to support caregivers. At least, not the invisible ones that land in the role. Not the young partners, the adult children, the friends who don't hide in crisis. There is no system for them. They get told they are strong instead of being asked if they are okay. There are no required welfare checks on them. There's just no culture of care for those who pour everything into caring for someone behind closed doors.

This isn't just true for our personal lives; I've seen it in the professional space too. There's no training required to become a support worker. There are no requirements for checking their psychological fitness. There's no overtime paid for taking someone's pain away while on shift and carrying it all home with you. I've offered care to people who were unwilling or unable to care for themselves. Sometimes, I worked under those who saw caregivers as replaceable; their acts were just seen as a job or a shift. And while some caregivers treat it as a job, my heart was what led me to care professionally, not my pockets. I worked under someone who valued their carers' presence but never their welfare. Demanded everything and offered little. The system is messy and there's so much that is built on the quiet sacrifice of its carers.

The message from Holly, although delayed, feels like a full-circle moment. Not only does it feel like an apology, but it feels like the hug I needed back then. It feels like the hug I needed from society. She has now lived some version of what I did and felt. She understood what it costs to give yourself completely; to pour when totally empty. That in itself brought me peace.

I hold Billie a little tighter, and feel her hug me just as I realise, I didn't write this story to recount what happened. I wrote it in memory of all that was missing. To offer what I didn't have. I wrote this for all those who have needed holding as they held someone else. For every silent sacrifice of a caregiver. Those who poured from an empty cup, being told they were strong rather than asked if okay. For all those who fell silent because it was too hard to be seen. Those in the hospital wards, the bedrooms, the stale kitchens, the quiet corners of the world, where care is given and not returned.

If that was you, or if this is you, I hope this book finds you randomly, dropped at your door with a casserole, too, as a reminder that your care matters. That you matter.

That, I've learnt, is the true art of giving. It's not about the coin toss between selflessness and survival. It's knowing that you matter too. And so I offer this book as another act of care; to all the givers who forgot to give back to themself. Please understand that in truly caring for others, you are not asked to vanish. You are invited to stay. Whole, seen, held and hugged.

You are not the cost of your kindness.

acknowledgements

Writing this book has, for the most part, been a joy. A way to finally set down some of the heaviness I once felt I carried alone.

But the truth is, I was never truly alone. I want to acknowledge the love and safety I've always had in my immediate family, especially my wonderful parents. I feel incredibly fortunate to have navigated early adulthood knowing I had the safest place to fall back - you two. I've always known you had my back, and that is an extraordinary privilege. To also have such kind, lovable, and inspiring role models is a gift beyond words. I hope you both know how deeply I look up to you, and that in my eyes, my parents really are the pick of the crop.

I know it scares you to see me so vulnerable in sharing this story. Thank you for your fierce protection, for caring so much, and for supporting me even when it feels frightening.

To Timmy B, thanks buddy/chief/champ/sport/muscles! You will always be my "happily ever after," and I'm so bloomin' glad our paths crossed when they did. Everything with you feels familiar, like we've walked through many lives together before. Taking risks and stepping into uncomfortable places... like publishing books or starting businesses! It all feels possible because I know at the end of the day there's a steady head, a laugh, and a full heart waiting for me. I'm endlessly thankful for your comfort, your encouragement, and all we will continue to create together.

Of course, the greatest thing you've given me, and our most wonderful creation yet, is our baby girl, Billie Sue. Thank you for refreshing our lives and being beyond our wildest, sweetest dreams. Billie, you are something truly special. I hope you live a life full of big, brave, and scary dreams. Whether that's writing books, singing pop hits, or whatever calls your heart. Your mum and dad will always be right behind you, cheering you on - even if it scares us, too.

To Tim's immediate and wider family, thank you for adopting me as your own. The love, warmth, and belonging you've shown me since moving to Taree is a gift I treasure deeply.

To my angels. All of my grandparents and my cousin Ash. I know you've kissed Billie a thousand times before she reached us, and I feel your fierce protection every single day.

And to our furry earth angel, Dot. Thank you for curling up beside me as I wrote, reminding me that sometimes the greatest lesson in love is simply being there, quiet and unconditionally.

To my circle of vibrant and adoring friends, my unstoppable cheer squad - there's no way to name you all, but please know how much you've carried me. Special mention goes to those who crossed my path at pivotal points and gave me exactly what I needed in that moment, leaving imprints I'll never forget. You believed in me more than I believed in myself.

A big shout-out to Vanessa Barrington, The Book Doula,

and her incredible community of writers. What a talented, inspiring bunch to walk alongside in this journey. Vanessa, thank you for every nudge, every word of guidance, and for believing in me and this story. This book wouldn't exist without you. You're bloomin' awesome.

To fellow caregivers and overgivers - those silently sacrificing so much for someone else. Please know it is never unnoticed. You are wildly important and deeply appreciated. Make sure you stop to smell the roses now and then, and take care of yourself. You can keep giving - but only if it comes from a place of joy. Spoiler alert: joy comes when you've cared for yourself first. I see you. This book is for you.

And finally, to you, the reader, thank you for holding my story gently in your hands. I hope it reminds you that your story matters, too.

about the author

Warm, creative, and deeply reflective, Karlee Hayes brings heart and honesty to everything she does. Based in the Manning Valley, New South Wales, she works remotely from home while raising her daughter and sharing the everyday joys of life as a builder's (almost) wife.

Her memoir, The Art of Giving, draws from her lived experience as a young carer and professional caregiver. With unflinching honesty, she explores the hidden costs of overgiving, the weight of burnout, and the courage it takes to rebuild an authentic life with balance.

Alongside writing, Karlee celebrates love stories as Your Smiling Celebrant, runs her eco-friendly gifting business Seed A Smile, and supports businesses through her role with a leading online booking platform. She is passionate about connection in all its forms - whether through ceremonies, seeds, or stories - and proves that even from the quiet corners of regional life, voices can carry far.

Readers are encouraged to connect with Karlee on Instagram @karleehayes and explore more of her work at www.karleehayes.com.au.

if you need support

Writing this book meant retracing some incredibly challenging times. If reading this stirs up heavy feelings for you, please know you are not alone, and there is help for you, too.

If you are ever in immediate danger, please call your local emergency number right away.

In Australia
- Lifeline — 13 11 14 (24/7 crisis support)
- Beyond Blue — 1300 22 4636 (mental health support)
- Kids Helpline — 1800 55 1800 (for young people 5–25)

Elsewhere
- U.S. — dial 988 (Suicide & Crisis Lifeline)
- U.K. & Ireland — Samaritans 116 123
- For other countries, please look up your local crisis hotline or search "suicide prevention helpline" in your region.

THE ART OF ~~LIVING~~ GIVING | 279

I also want to remind you that caring for your mental health is not reserved for the unwell, and shouldn't be left until crisis point. Looking after your mind is just as important as nourishing your body with good food or moving your body with exercise. Therapy can be a wonderful starting point - I personally value my regular check-ins with my therapist through BetterHelp, an accessible online option available from your phone.

May you always remember: even the darkest nights give way to morning light, and you are worthy of that bright new day x

www.ingramcontent.com/pod-product-compliance
Lightning Source LLC
Chambersburg PA
CBHW020520080526
44583CB00013B/678